The Art of Masturdating

The Art of Masturdating

A Guidebook for Single Heterosexuals

Helena B. Rich, L.C.S.W.

iUniverse, Inc.
New York Lincoln Shanghai

The Art of Masturdating
A Guidebook for Single Heterosexuals

iUniverse, Inc.

For information address:
iUniverse, Inc.
2021 Pine Lake Road, Suite 100
Lincoln, NE 68512
www.iuniverse.com

ISBN: 0-595-29257-7

Printed in the United States of America

Contents

SECTION 2: SEX

SECTION 3: MARRIAGE

ACKNOWLEDGEMENTS

I want to thank a number of people who have made this book possible. First and foremost, the people who assisted with the writing and editing of the book throughout my writing journey: Jennifer C., Marcie W., Donna F. Jackie K., Ken D., and John O. Thanks to all of you, with all my heart, for taking the time and energy to give me sound and constructive feedback and for all of the laughs we shared.

The many adventures that propelled me into actually writing the book warrant an acknowledgement. Those who were there with me or felt so inclined to "tell all," thank you! Jennifer C., Eun J., Lora B., Jackie K., Jeanette N., Tracy L., Erin P., Kim H., Ethan P., John O., Kevin D., Donna F., John K., Cordelia R., Meliss G., Christine C., Anji G., Dan D., Neville T., Andrea M., Sandi W., Howard F., Lisa R., Adam H., Jeff O., Jami R., Andrea S., Sam K.

A special thanks to Jennifer C., who, despite a number of simultaneous challenges, not withstanding a regular correspondence to edit from a different state, stayed with me during the crazy adventure of this first book. My heart truly goes out to you, for had you not kept up in the earlier stages of the book, I don't know how I would've gotten through it. And, of course, to Melissa M. who listened and listened to my stories when they were sad and frustrating and who also enjoyed them with me when they were comical and amusing. Your support has been tremendous. Thank you so much.

Had I begun the writing of the book at a later point, I would've had had a lot more material as a result of the following people who have come into my life: Deb S., Mike S., Asher P. and Jen C., Stephanie T, Rob W., and Gian T. This can only mean that I'll have to write a sequel. Though my stories may not have included you, Deb S., you are part of the book in spirit.

I'd like to acknowledge Rob W. for his support and encouragement as a fellow author and I so appreciate your attempts connect me with your agent despite the different genre of book. And, to David W. who gave me some very helpful constructive feedback as another fellow author and who attempted the same. I admire you both and your successes.

Most importantly, I want to thank my parents who, without their openness and support, I wouldn't have felt so willing and excited to write about such a subject matter. Your compassion and willingness to communicate from early on has been invaluable. And for the best sister one could wish for, Lora B. Your unconditional love and consistent support over the years has meant so much to me.

INTRODUCTION

Let me start by saying that this book should be dedicated to all of those amazing people out there that just so happen to be single. People have long asked the burning questions, "Why don't you have a boyfriend?" and "Why don't you have a girlfriend?" Many have made comments such as "I just don't understand it, you're such a catch" and "You must just be too picky" or "You just need to relax and it will happen—it happens when you least expect it." Then, you have the individuals who are well meaning, of course, making various suggestions like joining a club or doing things alone or telling friends and family that you are available. And, let's not forget the ones who say how young you are and how much time you have ahead of you. "You're such a baby." At what age, might I ask, *do* single men and women stop being seen as "such a baby?"

To keep the quest to meet "the one" in perspective, people have different experiences, different outlooks, and different approaches regarding all aspects of life, and meeting that "life partner" is only one of many life experiences. It just happens to be the focus for a lot of single adults because they share the concern of not meeting that special someone.

After discussing my experiences with my women friends and hearing of theirs over the years, I decided that these stories were not only memorable, but also precious and shouldn't be forgotten. This book has served that purpose and shares some curious tales with all of you.

It is my opinion that both women and men will be able to relate to at least one of these stories and that they will appreciate what the women referred to here have been through. I think that men will also gain not only more of an understanding of what a woman's experience is in the world, but also that they will be able to appreciate the female gender. It is my hope that everyone will be able to gain something from this book, whether a laugh, a cry, a shock, an education, or a deeper understanding of love and dating.

I believe it is important to explain that the purpose of this book is not to ostracize or humiliate men, but rather to assist men in developing their sense of the women species. Though you will also find some generalizations, they are in part to make a point. As with all generalizations, there are always exceptions. It is also a book of funny anecdotes and stories that should be shared and put to use, if only for someone to get a kick out of what constitutes the single lifestyle. Additionally, the book can be of assistance to women with respect to normalizing some of their experiences and consequently, helping them feel as if they're not alone. I say these things with both a humorous and analytical tone. I offer my comments and insights with love and humor. My fondness and fascination for people has propelled me to analyze the "dating world," a world that people often have strong feelings about. My intention is to entertain. I invite you to read further with a critical yet comical view. I hope to shed light on some of the untold realities of the single lifestyle, and to remove the blinders that people often wear.

As one might delineate from what's been said, this non-fictional semi-autobiographical book is written for the heterosexual population by a heterosexual author. To address the homosexual population would be to write a different book, as it is a different culture. Though some of the stories and suggestions may be of interest and/or assistance, it's only fair to respect the differences and be fair to the reader. So, don't feel you need to turn away from the book if you aren't straight, but be prepared for the tone if you do opt to read it. Additionally, though I don't promote frequent intoxication, this book includes a number of stories in which alcohol is referenced. If one is sober or doesn't drink or "party" for other reasons there may be less that one can relate to. I just want to recognize that there are differences within preferences, cultures, religion, and lifestyles and I recognize this book may not be for everyone. Even if you don't use substances, I still think there can be plenty you'll be able to relate to.

Lastly, I've decided to section the book into three parts: dating; sex; marriage. So, you, the reader, may find that you can benefit from and/or relate to one section better than the others. The subject matters are all intertwined but address very different concepts and are directed toward different people. Take what you want from the book, whether a great laugh, validation, or a bit of education.

SECTION 1:

DATING

1

HOW TO IMPRESS A WOMAN

It has been my experience that some men are just great catches and others want to appear as if they are. Those that just appear great have become adept at saying the "right" thing that they believe women want to hear. I sometimes wonder if there is a direct correlation between the frequencies with which a man tells you what you want to hear and how much T.V. he watches.

There are a variety of things a man can do to impress a woman. For example, if a man has certain books in plain view at his house (and he has actually read them), this can sometimes be a means of impressing her. Additionally, if a man has done some soul searching and he has worked on himself to some degree, this can be quite impressive to most women.

If a man asks questions and shows an interest when a woman responds, this is a true asset for the man. Conversely, if a man talks at length about himself and doesn't seem to really have the capacity to listen or explore what others have to say, this can be quite a turn-off.

The issue of knowing what one wants applies here also. For example, when a man is clear about what he wants to do for a date, and he is able to express this, this can be indicative of a man who is clear and stable. This never fails to impress a woman. When we look at men who continually say, "I don't know" or don't have a plan for the date, women deduce that he may not know a lot of things. When there is a question of what to do and a man answers regularly with, "I don't care," this can be a warning sign. If he doesn't care, then will he care about the direction in which the dating relationship is going? I do believe that decision-making is very important.

I would wager that there might be men who are trying to find the balance between making the decisions and giving the woman an opportunity to make decisions. If this is the case, I think it is something that a couple will figure out down the road. In addition, my friend, Jen recently dated a man a couple of times who constantly said, "I'm real flexible." Now, being really flexible is great but when mentioning your flexibility is your only response, one does wonder if the person is really being honest. Basically, one can sometimes draw a connection between what a man says with respect to daily issues and how it relates to him on a broader scale.

If a man wishes to impress a woman and he is well read, self aware, inquisitive, and clear, he will have very little difficulty. If he is also intuitive and can read personal cues to draw conclusions and make assessments, this also can be helpful. If a man is insincere, narcissistic and vague, but is aware of these flaws and willing to work on improving himself, then there is hope. Keep in mind that there needs to be an invested interest on the man's part in how he is experienced by women.

I think a man who actually *listens* to a woman when she is talking is a man who bears one of the most important personal attributes. This, of course, ideally, would have to begin with a man who is willing, interested, and able to ask the woman questions. Recently, I met a woman who shared about her dating experiences and the theme that persisted for her, as for so many other women, was that the men asked no questions.

Something else interesting to note is that men who have at least one sister are usually a bit more sensitive and aware of women's needs. This makes sense. Women with brothers also appear to have a better overall sense for men and this can at times impact their relationship potential with other men in a positive light. I think inquiring about the gender of a potential partner's siblings can be helpful. In addition, if a man treats his mother with respect and has a good relationship with her, there is a good indication that he is more likely than not capable of a quality relationship.

It has been my experience, time and time again, that women appear to gravitate to, and be taken with men who are out walking their dog. What is it? I think men with dogs are likely to be comfortable with responsibility and commitment and showing affection. The dog is truly a "chick magnet." I've considered getting a dog to test this theory because I love them and want to see how much of a conversation starter a dog could be. Essentially, if a person has some avenue in which to break the ice and facilitate a discussion, this can be the beginning to a very positive mating experience. I've heard that the likelihood of women choosing to talk to a man increases when he is with a dog. People are also inevitably approached more frequently when with a dog as opposed to when they are solo.

Interestingly enough, women are often very excited and enamored when they come across a man with a child. There is something about the soft nature of a man that can be seen when watching him show his loving and gentle side. I think, of course, when a woman is craving to reproduce with a man and they come into contact with just that, or a symbol of it, their clock ticks even more. I must admit this is a hook for me. On the flip side, however, if the child is quite young, the man is probably attached and then we can be left with the thought, "why not me, why not me?"

Despite the appeal of the softer side of men with children, there is a lot to be said for the "man's man" toughness. Men that have small or large scars that aren't extremely distracting or horrific looking are wearing a symbol of masculinity. In various conversations over the years with a number of my girlfriends, we have agreed that signs of masculinity are a major turn on. It is quite fascinating but it is indeed true. One girlfriend of mine shared with me about a man who had a dog bite scar on his face and how this totally turned her on. She pretty much made out with him just because of the scar. This is not to say that you single men should make a point to get a dog bite, but rather you should consider embracing and enjoying your scars rather than being embarrassed by them.

Lastly, if a man wishes to turn on a woman or make her feel taken care of and appreciated, a foot massage is always a sure thing…unless, of course, the woman feels uncomfortable about her feet…or if he does, for that matter. If one does something they truly aren't comfortable with in their heart, it is reflected somehow in the exchange. Watch for this when giving and receiving massages. For that matter, when oral sex is involved, the recipient may be able to tell with great ease as to whether or not the giver is truly interested in doing it. So, as a giver, I think it is useful to really consider if you are interested in what you're doing, because if you're not, it might even feel worse to the receiver than receiving nothing at all.

Black men deserve a lot of credit. I've had discussions with various friends of mine about this subject. First of all, black men have balls. If they're down, if they're interested, they are all over it. They come right out and say what they want to say. My friend and I discussed this very matter and she reminded me of a couple of very funny lines she's heard. Example 1: He says: You must be tired. She asks: Why? He says: Cause you've been running through my mind all day. Example 2: He asks: How are you? She says: Fine. He says: You sure are. I just love these examples of coy, flirty directness. So, may the Caucasian, Asian, or any other man take lessons from the Brother who just says it like it is.

On many occasions, my friends and I have been walking or talking when many a man approaches us to pay us a compliment. It is flattering to us and gutsy for them. I love it. And, unsolicited attention and compliments can pay off. They say flattery is the key to a man's heart. I'm not so sure this isn't also the case for women.

Years ago, I went dancing with some friends. I saw a guy there whom I had seen skating at the beach many times. He was adorable. And, boy, could he dance. So, I worked my way toward the area he was getting his "groove on" and proceeded to strut my stuff with my boogie shoes. One thing led to another, and we were getting down. He was hot, amazing, and great to dance with. Over the next five years, I only saw him periodically.

It wasn't until about two years ago that I was with two friends at the beach and we saw him. Both friends are gutsy and, unlike myself, will talk to anyone. One friend ultimately struck up a conversation with the hot guy and he turned out to be a nice guy. We ended up going into this local bar for a drink and to watch the sunset. What a shock!

So, we hang out and chat and his other friend was there. Then it was time to go, but not for all. He proposed we hang out a little longer. I couldn't argue with that. We then went back to my apartment, proceeded to get "shit-faced" and, you guessed it, had a wild night of awesome sex. It was just amazing. It was all over the house. What helped was a mutual admiration for slow black fuck music and old school funk. The funny thing was that he had a woman's car. I guess he was seeing her but not seriously. He left with candied lube all over his post-sexed body.

He called a few days later. We made plans to hang out. All the while, I'm struggling with my own morals, sexuality, and realism. I think he wanted a cheap lay because he came over with no money. We ordered food, I get him stoned, and we drank some wine. We get so stoned that it had the adverse effect on me sexually. I was not feeling very motivated to get down and dirty. I thought to myself, why put any effort into someone sexually if they don't mean anything to you? I felt as if I'd just rather lie there, while he does his thing, and while I do nothing. He ultimately left, disappointed, blue balls, and all…he tucked me in bed and bid me farewell. I haven't seen him since. He sure was *fine* though.

Another point for most other cultures and/or ethnicities is that women's body hair doesn't trip them out. They don't seem to have much of an issue about it. And, to top it off, they like an ass and some meat on a woman's bones. This is where the white dudes need to get a clue.

2

HOW TO IMPRESS A MAN

Knowing the men that I have over the years, both as friends and as lovers, it is quite simple for them to list the various ways in which a woman can be appealing. This is of course true for the more manly man, and the man who may be a bit more traditional and independent. Men who are less independent or less traditional or more feminine may have more of a struggle with what is very clearly appealing to them due to their own less "fixed" world or views. A woman who is into sports, both as a spectator and as a participant, can sometimes be a real convenience and a turn on. If she exercises/works out and doesn't present herself in such a way that she may be misperceived as a "butch" lesbian, it's all the better. If she's the non-jealous type and doesn't mind if her guy goes "out with the guys" (with the flexibility of a strip club) on a Saturday night for example, she's considered a "real winner."

Then we have the woman who will have an orgasm without faking it and the woman who loves oral sex, both as a giver and as a receiver. Generally, these are very appealing qualities women can have. Top it off with a woman who likes beer and doesn't broach the subject of marriage or commitment, the man feels he's sort of home free. And, lastly, if she's a good driver (men are known to be "better" drivers than women) and has interests of her own, she may really be considered top notch.

The reality is that every dating scenario offers a different dynamic. These "turn-ons" may be true for some men, while not for others, just as the case is true about women's attraction toward men. Ultimately, two people connect despite some less appealing traits or a lack of some of the more appealing ones.

3

WHAT NOT TO DO

It appears that men sometimes don't realize the ramifications of their behavior because they fail to see the fundamental and distinct differences between men and women. I think that women tend to focus more on how a man will see, interpret, and respond to her behavior than a man does when interacting with a woman. The following list are some suggestions that I've gathered from women friends of mine that can be cause for a chuckle, or better yet, something applicable to one's life:

A. A man should never leave a condom sticking out of his wallet on the second date. Doing so could be perceived as presumptuous and/or tacky. This actually happened to my girlfriend Jen. The guy showed up at her house and propositioned her in the living room in broad daylight. He said, "I have this," referring to an extra-large sized condom. He made no effort to disguise it. The funny thing is that he really didn't need the extra large. He must have really been feeling confident and secure in his maleness all around.

B. A man should never let a condom fall out of his sock prior to any agreement being made regarding having intercourse. Seems a bit presumptuous. I have heard this story from not one woman but two. Maybe their partners used thick wool socks for more than warmth. Both incidents occurred in the midwest and it's a bit cooler there than in Los Angeles. Neither of the women anticipated having sex that night. The lesson here is be a bit more slick. Heck, maybe the men I have been with were so damn slick that I had no idea they retrieved the condoms we used from their socks.

C. A man should not send group emails with 50 women's names on them when he is pursuing someone new. Jen described to me an experience when she received a group e-mail. We decided that, although men should be encouraged to have women friends, it feels awkward for a woman on the group email when she doesn't know if all the other women are just friends with the man. One then starts to wonder if the man is dating or has dated the other women. The suggestion would be to not include new conquests on a group e-mail list.

D. A man should not make a CD with love songs and give it to a woman on the second date. My friend Eve actually had this experience. Essentially, this can be a bit excessive at first, and though it is a nice gesture that I think most woman would appreciate, it needs to be put on hold so as not to overwhelm the woman or contribute to any feelings of suffocation. My suggestion, which the woman who got the love song CD also supported, would be to give a flower or a card or express that he had a nice time and save the CD for a few dates later.

E. A man should never have a photo of himself on an Internet date site, legs crossed, holding a teacup with a pinkie raised if he is in hopes of meeting a woman. Although this may be a comfortable position for him, it appears feminine to any woman looking for that "masculine man." Don't get me wrong, I am not saying this is bad, but a less manly appearance sometimes doesn't work as well for a first impression. Similarly, a woman in some masculine pose may be less appealing to a man searching for a really feminine woman.

F. A man should never, in an attempt to be passionate and expressive early on in a relationship, say to a woman, "I'm *fucking* nuts about you." Recently, I went out to a bar with my sister Madison, her friend Megan, and my girlfriend Jess. Megan described the story as it had happened to her the week before. So, I wrote it down on a napkin (that was all I had at the time) so as to remember the story for the book. I wrote it down and left it on the bar counter. Then a man walks up and looks down and sees the napkin. I immediately grab it, chuckling and feeling a bit awkward. He knew it wasn't meant for him but we all laughed at the idea of leaving this suggestion for someone to pick up.

G. A man should never continue to talk to a woman and follow her around when she has given no indication that she is at all interested in him. This constitutes stalking. This lesson about "what not to do" was brought home to me when I took a trip with Eve to Mexico. A man we met was clearly interested in the ladies, hooking up, and making friends. Well, he was an excessive talker, a bit annoying, and completely clueless. He didn't pick up on the vibe that he wasn't wanted. Unfortunately, the night he stalked us was the first of many and he became known as "the stalker," and the one that everyone needed to avoid. He was a nice guy, but so desperate that you throw a few drinks in him and he's unstoppable.

4

ACRONYMS AND NICKNAMES

Acronyms can be such an enjoyment for those who use them. Essentially, when there is an incident, a situation, or something of note, it can help to use an acronym so as to conveniently be able to make a quick reference in the future. Some of the acronyms listed below may seem derogatory but they are intended to just be humorous.

SLM—single lonely men—I chose this term a few years back to describe what seemed to be a common theme for the men I met when I went out with friends. There seemed to be a lot of men with somewhat sad looking demeanors, not necessarily feeling good about themselves, or so it appeared, and clearly wishing, despite at least a moderate amount of insecurity, that some woman would give them the time of day. There appeared to be a sense of desperation we picked up on in their presence; this desperation became something we definitely felt we had to avoid…the SLM. So, when we go to a bar and see this we can quickly make a comment about it and choose to stay or to go, depending on our mood of course. Actually, an SLM might be a good thing, depending on how you look at it.

SBF—simulated butt fucking—a number of years ago, while in college, a friend of mine had a very unusual experience with a friend of hers. Essentially, they were attracted to one another but neither person had ever taken the initiative to pursue something further. One day, she finally broke the ice and brought the concept of sleeping together up to him…he thought this might be a good idea, as long as they both were clear about expectations and circumstances. Finally, one night, he went over to her house and they opted to swap massages. He began. He disrobed her from the waist up and began massaging. He was fully clothed. After a short period of time he then began to thrust into her butt area as if they were having anal sex. Not long after this awkward and unusual maneuver he came in his pants…it was then that a new acronym was evolved…SBF.

SBFM—slow black fuck music—yet again another term in which I think most understand. There are many songs that seem to put you in "the mood" and all I can say is that it is very fortunate. In essence, who doesn't need a little help at some times…and what better music than this to set the mood. If you're wondering what in the heck I'm referring to, I'm talking about Maxwell, Marvyn Gaye, Luther Vandross, and others in the R&B genre.

DC—dork central—this term was coined when a friend of mine and I went to visit another friend at a restaurant while watching a Lakers game. There we were, not necessarily looking for love but maybe someone with whom we could flirt…we both looked at each other after some time had passed and agreed that there were a lot of people who were sort of dorky. Hence, the term DC was coined. Fortunately we have had to use the term only once since that evening.

LS—love spice—this term was coined in about 1987, while I was in high school…essentially it has a few meanings. First, it can be used as an adjective to describe when a woman is really feeling an intense attraction to someone, and they experience a certain heat, and become all consumed with the man. Second, it can be used as a verb to describe when one is flirtatious and giddy. Third, it can be used an adjective to describe when someone is really interested in someone else and has that glassy-eyed excited feeling.

HMF—horny mother fucker—this term is self-explanatory. Usually this is used toward someone who is either a friend or someone who is drunk and leaning on you, trying to pick up on you…so, it can be used as a fun joking term to a good buddy or, as a way of summing up negative perception of a person who is so horny, it is annoying.

FMR—fuck me red—generally, this term is used to describe the color of lipstick or nail polish. What type of red is this? It's dark, and makes a statement. So, FMR is used to describe the come hither mindset. For example, "She was wearing FMR lipstick and was hot to trot." Or, I was feeling a bit scandalous and decided to wear some FMR nail polish.

RA's—Random Assholes—This is a helpful term when one has negative feelings about people because of the way they are behaving. An example of this might be when one is frequenting bars or something of the sort, and everyone seems to be unpleasant in one way or another. Though this term is negative and we don't use it often, it is nice to be able to say RA without anyone having a clue as to what is being referenced.

Gumby—This term came from a funny experience that a girlfriend of mine had in her younger years. She was at a party with some older people from the local college. She and this young college student about 3 years her senior really hit it off. They end up deciding to fool around a little bit and they went into one of her friend's bedrooms. She gave him head. When she was done, he exclaimed, "Holy shit, oh my god, look at what you did!" She was completely horrified and puzzled, because her former boyfriend had complimented her blowjob technique. The man then showed her the gum he had all throughout his pubic hair. He was embarrassed as hell because he knew he'd have to shave it and, he was on a swim team so this was something that wouldn't go unnoticed. She must have forgotten she had gum in her mouth. From that point on, how could she not be called Gumby?

Flover—a friend or loved one perceived sexually. This term appropriately was added to our vocabulary when a dear friend was stewing and love spicing over a man-friend of hers. Our other friend then referenced him as a "flover." Dumfounded, the smitten friend asked what she was talking about, to which she replied, "He is a friend or loved one perceived sexually."

5

NAMING MEN

Naming men can be empowering and quite hysterical. I encourage men to give their dates a name for common reference as well. I actually have a friend who tends to do this so frequently that I often don't know what the true names are of the men who she is referring to. I have to admit, I love it.

A man who I dated briefly earned a name after we'd broken up. My girlfriend Sasha and I worked out at the same gym as he. Granted, people shouldn't have to be concerned about how they look at the gym, nor should they have to be worried about what others are saying or thinking, but we just couldn't help ourselves. When he did abdominal crunches, he somehow curled up and looked like a monkey. His nickname became "monkey man."

My girlfriend Joy and I were at the beach recently and noticed a man with binoculars. We wondered what he was doing with them. We continued to watch him and realized he used them to check out women. Ogling women with binoculars seems quite intrusive, especially at a place like the beach when you can see so much skin anyway. Not a good thing. He became the "bino dude" for the rest of the day.

In the recent past I dated an ex-baseball player. He peppered most of his conversation with references to baseball. He lied about his age, telling people he was five years younger than he was. He said that was his "baseball age," and he even shaved his pubes a particular way that he said players did. In addition, he would use his baseball connections to get a variety of perks when we would go out. After we dated, I learned he never actually played in the big leagues. Because he was a person whose identity was so falsely wrapped up in baseball, he earned the name "Mr. Baseball." I don't have a recollection if he ever learned of this nickname, but I'm sure if he had, he would probably have appreciated it. This would have been contraindicated of course.

Jen, with whom I share a fondness for nicknames, met a man at a singles event. She described him as quite tall, with a real presence. What was seemingly the most impressive and outstanding quality of this person were his hands. Though I was never an actual witness to his hands, she had described them as some of the largest hands she'd ever seen. We all know what that means…he doesn't have his birth name but rather, "Big Hands."

Jen had also been involved with a different man a couple of years back. He had seventeen body piercings, which some may feel is a turn-on. For her, it was most definitely a turn-on. After about one date in which they hung out, she keyed the phrase, "Metal Man." Though I never had the opportunity to meet Metal Man, I always felt I had a solid picture of what he looked like. This is clearly one of the benefits to nicknames—anyone you tell can get a picture of the individual even if they have never met the person.

Eve and I, on our trip to Mexico, met one man who was very aloof and sarcastic. Unbeknownst to a number of people is the fact that sarcasm can be a way in which anger manifests itself. So, after a couple of cocktails and conversation at a table of about ten, this man continued to come across as angry in his comments. We then decided that "Angry Man" was quite fitting for him.

6

HOW ABOUT THE MEN IN UNIFORM?

The Instructor fetish-We can't deny that men who are in teaching roles are often found to be attractive. There is something about the knowledge, the wherewithal, and the power that comes with being an instructor. And, to add to that, if the instructor pays special attention to you, well, that can definitely send your mind spinning. I once felt a mutual attraction with a self-defense instructor of mine who wore an athletic uniform for the martial arts school. His name was Mark. He appeared to be flirting, and he had a sharp wit. A clever wit, for me, is extremely attractive. I developed a curiosity about him. Jess was a mutual friend and one day after class we were discussing our plans for the day. I didn't have any prior engagements and he had plans to go to a driving range. Well, I had been interested in learning how to play golf (to meet men, of course). Jess suggested that Mark and I go together.

It took everything I had to contain myself and keep my composure. I casually agreed and we decided to meet within the half hour at the range. It was then that I realized I was only fueling the fire seeing as he would, once again, be in that darn instructor role. He gave me some good tips and we shared a little about ourselves. After finishing, he proposed that we go grab a beer, and so we did at a little hole in the wall nearby. After golfing, beer drinking, and connecting, it seemed to me that there was indeed something there.

Not long after this, I invited him dancing with some other friends. Note that when we had been in the bar I used his phone to check my home machine. I have caller ID, which meant that, when I got home I had his number. We danced the night away and even without his uniform, one thing led to another, and we ended up spending the night together and fooling around.

This was both a good and a bad thing. Unfortunately, I'd had too much to drink and wasn't able to appreciate that we'd been able to hook up. However, I had the impression that this might mean it could happen again. We didn't have sex and seeing as he seemed like a respectful guy, I hoped to talk with him again and spend some time together. This took some time but ultimately there was an event in which we were together as a group and again he and I went home together. This time we had phenomenal sex. Not long afterwards he invited me for a drink, which ended up in another night of wild passionate sex. It was during this last incident that we really seemed to connect, more so than before. What I realized was that he truly was not interested despite the initial sense that I had about him. I ultimately had to let this one go, despite the uniform and all.

One very interesting aspect of this story is that it debunks the idea that having a fuck buddy with no commitment is every man's dream. When I realized, for whatever reason, that Mark was not interested in pursuing something with me, I figured I had a couple of choices. One choice was to let it go, the other was to see what happened, and the third was to propose a "friends with benefits" relationship. We had had sex and it was good, he wasn't a stranger, he lived close by, he wasn't looking for a relationship, there was no one on the horizon for me, and we were both consenting adults. Put 2 and 2 together. Why not have a purely sexual relationship? I mean, it seemed ideal, with all of the ducks in a row. Interestingly, I think when I proposed this to him it freaked him out. He expressed discomfort with the idea to which I sincerely respected our difference. But, I do think that most men wouldn't turn down an agreement like this unless they are not attracted to the woman or if she intimidates him.

The Navy Man Fetish—A number of years ago, I had the pleasure of meeting another man in uniform, a Navy Seal named Cody. What I learned, after knowing him for a short period of time, was that Navy Seals are crazy. If you consider the number of things they have to endure and the level of secrecy of what they do, it is no wonder they are a bit on the edge. All that aside, there is something to be said for the macho-like, extremely athletic, and savior-type man.

I was extremely intrigued when I would hear Cody's vague stories about his work. He never broke the honor code The Seals have about secrecy. I felt a sense of safety being in his presence. We met while swimming laps in the pool at my girlfriend's condo. We began talking and it was a connection from the get go. I will never forget him providing me with my most scandalous and memorable sexual experience ever. He didn't have transportation at the time so he instructed me to meet him at the Naval Base. He had given me specific directions as to where to park and that he'd meet me, secretly, at that location. We met next to his barracks. The other team members were out at the time, so Cody led me inside. He began flattering me with compliments about my body and my outfit. Before I knew it, we were having sex right there in the locker room. No one other than Seal Team members are allowed on base. The fact that our rendezvous was so illicit made for an exciting sexual experience.

We dated for a while and kept in touch a while after. It turns out that he believed that he should be a gigolo and utilize his sexual ability and his huge dick to please women worldwide. His goal amused me, but also made sense. Everyone needs to have a sense of conquering the world, wants to be fearless, and carries a certain level of egocentricity. Unfortunately, we lost touch and I wasn't able to find out if he followed the gigolo career path. I will say, however, that I feel fortunate and flattered to have been able to satisfy my Navy man fetish.

My girlfriend Lizbeth had a cousin who studied at the Naval Academy. She was lucky enough to attend his graduation and was immersed in that community for a short time on her trip. To this day, Lizbeth will reference those Navy boys in their uniforms and how sexy they were. I think the appeal of the uniform may have been, in part, the reason why the film, *An Officer and A Gentleman* did so well and why I, like many other women, liked it so much.

The Lifeguard fetish—Lifeguards and red shorts function just as well as uniforms for most women. Hollywood knows this. Although the predominant feature on "Baywatch" is the hot babes, there are also a lot of men traipsing around in their red shorts. Again, the appeal seems to be the sense of feeling saved by someone. Lifeguards are trained to rescue and this can provide a sense of safety to women. When I was a lifeguard a number of years back, the most exciting part was purchasing that red bathing suit. It felt sexy to wear it. Every time I see a man in red shorts, I go wild. I don't know if this particular fetish is contained to those who live near the beach, or if it extends to the broader population, but regardless, the red shorts are sexy. I did once hear that red symbolizes sex. No wonder the red FMR nail polish usually works and red lifeguard shorts turn women on.

The Surfer fetish—I think this differs from the lifeguard fetish in that women don't detect the rescuer sense but more a mellow, serene, strong, and a bit wild appeal. Surfing is dangerous, takes dedication, and is a straight out turn on.

The Manly Man—My friends and I have for as long as I can remember discussed the level of turn on by a man who whittles. If a man can make, build, and create things out of wood or some other material, he is very appealing. I wonder if some biological instinct innate in women makes whittling and fixing things attractive. I think that the concept of men as hunters and providers is the root of this fetish. If men can provide for and make things for a home, they seem capable and sexy. Being a good handyman takes dedication, patience, creativity, and motivation. The same is true for fixing things. This is not to say that women are not capable of home improvement, but if a man can do these things, it sure makes things a hell of a lot more convenient.

The Fireman fetish—I have to say that I am fortunate enough to have been on a blind-double date with a fireman…unfortunately, I wasn't very attracted to him and he wasn't attracted to me. We only met the one time. Many of my girlfriends and I share that intrigue and curiosity about the men in the big red trucks. Is it something about the hoses, the red, the bulky uniforms, or something about them being rescuers and doers of good? Firemen have a downside though. A psychologist friend of mine once told me that firemen who undergo psychological testing commonly are found to be both narcissists and bed-wetters. I've also heard from fire experts that there is a correlation between fire setters or kids who are curious about fires and firemen.

Because a narcissist, in simplistic terms, is someone with an inflated ego, it would seem logical that being a fireman either worsens this tendency and/or attracts this type of person. This is not to say that all who are firemen are all narcissists. This is just something to keep in mind as a possibility and a potential warning sign. If only I could expand on the specifics about the bed-wetting. Maybe, again, there is some connection with the hose. Regardless, whether it is the color of the truck, what the truck contains, or the truck itself, women will always take a second glance when they see a fire truck making its way down the street. Maybe I should burn a little something so that I have some ashes that need to be double-checked.

One last tidbit to mention here: Sasha has long awaited the time that she can use some of her best fireman lines. "I could really use some help with your hose seeing as I'm real hot and need my fire to be put out," "I am ready to stop, drop, and roll," or "I have a fire underneath my skirt." I encourage a bold woman to do this…I have yet to have the opportunity. Best of luck to anyone who does.

Lizbeth had an opportunity to go on a date with a police officer. He had been investigating and following up on an incident that occurred on her parents' block. Of course, she had seen him from afar and thought, hey, he is a cutie in his police officer outfit. They went to dinner and then back to his house to listen to CD's. Unfortunately, my friend decided when she saw him in regular clothes, not *a'la'costume*, that he walked like a duck. This gait was a turn off that she couldn't get past. I think what is important here is to acknowledge that the uniform is a costume; it feeds into that unconscious desire we have for what is powerful, symbolic of "good," or represents manliness, safety or giving.

Jess and I went to Jamaica a couple of years ago and developed a trapeze artist fetish. As bizarre as it may sound, we were taken with the men performing in the circus. It was shocking how capable and phenomenal they were. Their bodies were cut to perfection (yes, like a piece of meat) and we immediately developed a fetish. I told her it was a must that we take some photos with them, seeing as they were so amazing looking. To this day, I've never thought of the circus in the same light. And, maybe it is good I've not come into contact with any more trapeze artists. God knows what might come over me.

7

DRESSING PROTOCOL

Clothing contributes to first impressions. The female fondness for men in uniform is only one of many images. Some men like the librarian look, the Catholic schoolgirl look, etc. I think it is interesting to talk with people about what bothers them and what appeals to them. Everyone has preferences of sorts, whether it is specific to a style of dress, a specific article of clothing, or the way in which a person presents him/herself.

A number of friends of mine and I have talked about men in flannel and faded jeans…the man who whittles, the man who is rugged and who represents the mountains or building things…the man who represents manliness. There is a "J.Crewishness" about him and he looks as though he lives in Montana, Idaho, New Mexico, Ohio, Arizona, or something of that sort. Chances are, he most likely does live in one of these places…or, maybe Northern California. Did I add that he drives a truck and has at least one dog?

Now, if we are on the subject of this "mountain-man," it is important to clarify the issue of cowboy hats and cowboy boots. If a man is a cowboy and this makes up his personality, then he is entitled to wear a cowboy hat and/or boots. If, however, he is just wearing them around (especially in L.A.), this is not okay. Is this true for women? I have heard various opinions about this from men. I think women are fortunate in that they can get away with more (at least in a man's eyes). Not long ago, I was at a restaurant/bar with some friends and we saw a true cowboy sitting at the bar. He had a *Miller Lite* in hand, *was smoking Marlboros*, wore cowboy boots, a flannel, a giant belt buckle, jeans that were not too baggy nor too tight, and of course, the cowboy hat. We found him quite appealing. So did the two women who were coming on to him.

Foreign men, on the other hand, often do not have the same sex appeal in their attire. Being foreign can be both appealing and a turn off depending on the whole package. For example, an accent can often be appealing. However, wearing the super tight pants that are popular in *your* country can be a major turn off elsewhere. My friend Keri met a hot Brazilian man in the Jacuzzi at her apartment complex. They hit it off and he asked her out on a date. When he arrived at her apartment, she was stunned…he was not only wearing tight pants, but he was also wearing black shoes with white socks. Bad foreign dressing can be difficult to deal with. It reminds me of a *Seinfeld* episode in which Elaine meets a man whom she thinks is great. She learns, soon after they meet, that he has a sixth toe. Despite all of her efforts, she was unable to get over it. Fortunately for my friend no surgery was required to help her Brazilian boyfriend. He has, with the advice of his friends, ditched the tight pants and is color coordinating his shoes and socks. The exception is the black tennis shoe.

Another friend of mine, Julie, went on a date with a big black man. When he arrived to pick her up, she almost lost it. He was wearing a Charlie Brown shirt and tennis shoes with slacks. Basically, it was a mix-match of the person and the outfit.

With all that has been said, it seems only fair to say that men shouldn't wear cowboy boots unless they are a cowboy or something of the sort, and black socks shouldn't be worn with white shoes, or vice versa.

A while ago, I dated a guy named Shane who mentioned to me he found Birkenstocks to be extremely unattractive, not at all sexy, and a reminder of the "grunge, hippie look." The funny part of all of this is that during our conversation he never asked if I owned a pair. We talked about the stereotypical hippie woman who doesn't shave or wear deodorant and doesn't brush her hair or paint her toes. He actually said, "My dick won't go anywhere near that." Now, I'd attended, as he knew, a school in which there were a lot of hippies, so we did discuss that. I shared that I'd never swayed too much in that direction and that I wasn't really the "hippie type."

The following time we met up the conversation resurfaced. He asked, "Did I ever ask you if you actually owned a pair of Birkenstocks?" I chuckled and told him no. He then asked, "Well, do you?" I thought for a second and told him to guess. And, because he's pretty insightful, he said, "I think you do but you don't want to tell me you do." I thought that was pretty good and then said, "I think I'm just going to make you wonder." Well, that didn't last long because he warned me that he'd play the game back. So, I told him the truth, that I have had a pair for about 10 years and that I generally don't wear them out and about but rather if I need to run outside for a minute or something. I only mention this scenario because it sheds light on the fact that everyone has their funny little things about attire and I was glad to be on the other side for a minute. It did leave me wondering how many other men have this feeling about Birkenstocks.

8

DATING PERSPECTIVES

Eve recently exclaimed, "Dating is not for the meek." This woman in particular comes from a traditional Korean household and has been set up on more dates than anyone else I've ever known. It is amazing what this woman has endured. What is interesting is, in her biculturalism, she is quite Americanized. Dating has been a struggle for her because she is most attracted to Jewish men, not Koreans.

It has been quite curious to me as to what the connection is to Jewish men specifically. Additionally, I also had a conversation recently with a Jewish man who was remarking on a friend of his who is "afflicted." This friend has an affiliation toward Asian woman and has just begun to date one. We conversed at length about this and I maintain, to which he seemed to agree in part, that there indeed is an element of appeal due to the fantasy of the woman being not only meek but also exotic. Maybe in a few decades we will have a great deal more Asian Jews. That would be interesting.

In Eve's years of dating numerous men, she always went out on three dates before she mad a final decision. She really advocated for giving people a chance. This did seem to work for her, though she hasn't made it past three dates for the past, oh, ten years.

What is it with the number three? A lot of common folklore about dating involves the number three. Go on three dates. Don't call for three days. Discuss threesomes because this may be a turn on to a man. Try to date three people simultaneously if you can, etc., etc, etc. Joy was recently juggling three men. Joe was very interested in her, was a nice guy and looking for a commitment. Kent was a nice, fun guy whom she had seen twice and slept with; she hadn't heard from him in a while. Dillon was someone she had met and connected with, talked with a lot on the phone and had a couple of dates with; he had not called. When this was all going on, I told her she had the perfect situation. She had someone she was giving the "three date chance" to, she had someone to satisfy her in bed sexually if she felt horny, and then she had the one she was really interested in. The risk of sabotaging something or becoming confused, frustrated, or over analytical, were minimized.

Now, this is the true definition of juggling. The funny thing is that I'd dated a man, Tyler (A.K.A. Mr. Baseball), for about six months who never made a commitment to me and always had excuses as to why. But, he always said, "I don't juggle." It was such a contradiction because he also wasn't committing to me, and he was leaving his options open. I think when someone repeatedly tells you the same line like, "I don't juggle" or, "I am very honest" that one should beware. Now I know that those expressions might mask dishonesty and a fear of commitment. How much explaining, justification, and commenting needs to happen on the one end to convince the other person? Actions speak louder than words.

One of the things I did learn from my time with Tyler is that different religions, cultures, ethnicities, politics, and upbringings combined can make for some serious difficulties. A number of men and women can most likely relate to this.

I tend to be picky, but I decided to try to open my mind a bit to let someone else in. He didn't fit the mold of the "ideal man" for me but there were a lot of things about him that were appealing, attractive, and endearing. Towards the end of our tryst, we took a month off for reflection and during this time I actually spoke with a number of people in marriages to ask about the compromises they'd made. I think I was looking to normalize our differences and determine if I felt the relationship was something workable. It turns out we had too many differences. He was much too conservative for me and there were a lot of double standards implied in our relationship.

In my hunt for differences with couples I'd known, I found a number of examples. I have a Jewish liberal woman friend who married a Catholic conservative man and she decided to convert for child rearing purposes. I have a Jewish man friend who married a Catholic woman and they are raising their children bi-religiously and celebrate all of their holidays. Another girlfriend of mine, who was raised on a more spiritual level and who knew how to party, married a man who was raised Mormon and had never had a sip of alcohol. A girlfriend of mine married a man a number of years younger than she who had no stable income when they met. Another girlfriend is in a long-term relationship with a man who already has a child from his previous marriage and they live 30 minutes away from one another. The reality is that compromises are often made on various levels. Some couples may choose to compromise on certain issues, while not on others. Ultimately, it depends on the commitment, priorities, and compatibility in the relationship.

Another issue that surfaces in courtship is when to have the "dating" discussion. For example, depending on how two individuals meet, there may be a discussion the very first night about what each person is expecting. In set-up dates and Internet dating and singles events, people tend to be more clear and frequently discuss hopes and intentions. If people are very direct, don't juggle, are looking for something serious, and don't play the dating game, they may then have the "what are we doing" conversation early on.

There is also the more ambiguous situation, which personally makes me go nuts. This is the, "take it slow, don't talk about it, let things happen, be patient" attitude. This is challenging because anxieties do then tend to arise in early dating and cause a great deal of frustration. This is why dating more than one person at a time can be quite valuable. It is a difficult feat to express and be interested in someone and not place any pressure on that person.

An additional tool that I have learned about is the "light" exercise. This is an exercise that can be helpful for some who don't necessarily trust their judgment or instinct and for some who like to have some structure in the dating process. Three (oh, there we go again!) columns are laid out, one for green lights, one for yellow lights, and one for red lights. Under these columns one writes down specifics about potential partners. For example, to use an extreme and cynical example to make the point easily…under the green column would be someone with the following qualities: friendly, intelligent, successful, self actualized, looking to develop a relationship and have a family. Yellow light column might consist of: drinks a lot more than I do, has changed jobs a lot, already has a child from a previous marriage, has a warrant out for his arrest due to multiple unpaid parking tickets. Red lights may be: has no job right now, isn't sure if he wants to start a family, doesn't get along with any of my friends, has murdered someone in the past five years. I know, for example, that I tend to be drawn toward the man who I'm trying to figure out and this can be dangerous. I need to be cognizant of this and consider it a yellow light.

This exercise can actually be very helpful because not only does it assist a person to be clear about his/her priorities, but it also forces one to pay attention to them and to have a guideline for him/herself. I encourage anyone to try this. Use it if it works, and don't if it doesn't. Everyone's list of qualities will be different. This is not meant to be rigid and all should feel as though they can change their lists at any given time. After all, we all do change and, as a result, so can our priorities.

One of the main benefits I have felt to being out there in the dating world is being exposed to a variety of restaurants and bars. These are places that I might not have gone to with just a friend or a family member for one reason or another. I must say that I can think of a number of places that I've been taken to on a date where I now go pretty frequently...and for that I'm thankful to the men who originally took me there. Men and women both should not forget to keep this in the back of their minds when going out on dates. Seize the opportunity to try new places. If anything, one will walk away having found a new venue he/she can return to later.

In talking with my co-worker, Kent, who is really enjoying his 30's, I learned of a very different perspective, that of he and his close friends. He has named himself the "white devil." You have to wonder what the heck this could mean. Basically, he explained to me that they have 5 strikes against themselves. Well, it just so turns out that he and a couple of his close friends represent the "true minority" as he states it: they are single, heterosexual, Caucasian, male, in their 20's and 30's. I think it is humorous that one can shift the perspective so that they feel/appear ostracized when 4 of the qualities are what others would deem privileged. He is determined to see himself as what everyone doesn't particularly like, hence "devil." I just found this to be hysterical. For some, it may also seem true.

This leads to another valuable point. Men who are in their 30's, who are not opposed to marrying, seem to be hooking up with women in their 20's. Time and time again, I'm hearing of people doing this. I have two male friends, with whom I went to school, who are essentially married. It leaves us women wondering if in fact those of us in our 30's will need to rethink where we're looking for love. Do we need to look into the idea of being with men in their 40's? I mean, what a concept. I don't think it is all that bad, however, seeing as the men who are interested in commitments seem to be far beyond their 30's in general.

This brings up the idea of last names and relationships, relating again to the concept of who wears the pants in the relationship. Last names taken by the women is a true representation of history and the idea of men wearing the pants and keeping the lineage intact. So, with that said, what is one to do if there are no more men with a last name who are reproducing? This is something that is happening in my family for example. Here we have two women (my sister and I), the last with our last names. Do we keep them? Do we hyphenate them? Do we combine them? Does it matter? I guess this is one of those things that people can have a strong feeling or opinion about yet there are many things one cannot predict. So, we leave this up to the pair when they are presented with what to do. The irony is that I never particularly liked my last name and growing up I would fantasize about how any other last name would be appealing. Now, I question what I will do when the time comes.

It was about three years ago when I met a man from Big Bear, California named Tony. It was at this time that I felt curious in learning more about my astrological map. I had heard about having a chart done before but wasn't sure if I'd actually agreed with this. I found a woman's name and tracked her down. I learned that it is actually a science and that one can determine a great deal based solely on exactly where and when they were born. I thought, heck, why not. She did my chart, knowing nothing about me really, and it was truly amazing what she told me. Things as simple and individualized as driving fast, being fidgety, loving animals and needing warm weather were only some of my traits accurately depicted. It did also paint sort of a picture that I shouldn't be with the Big Bear man, despite my intense attraction toward him. Here is my advice: try it before you knock it. After all, she had never met me and drew all of these accurate conclusions. It instilled a bit of hope in me because of the way in which things were reinforced that I may have been uncertain or on the fence about. I think in terms of psychic or tarot readings, these are not as concrete but more abstract rather. Admittedly, I've done a couple of these but never really got anything major or profound out of them, though I've heard of other's experiences being different.

In conversations with friends, family, and even in both sides of therapy, the concept of negative thinking and tunnel vision has often come to the stage. A girlfriend at work, who has never been to therapy, asked me one day where I was going. I told her I was going to therapy. She asked me why and I said, "I'm going so that I can be comfortable with the fact that I may not meet someone and that I may never get married or have kids." It seems so odd to spend money to do such a thing but I don't want to be walking around feeling bitter.

I think the most important fact I've learned is that being bitter or negative is not productive. The reality is that we (those looking for love, or hoping for it while not looking) need to not focus on the negative. We need to be hopeful, and positive, not be narrow-minded, and maintain a balance of all of these perceptions while being realistic at the same time. This, I believe, is the most insanely difficult task. The only individual that can really truly understand this balancing routine, as I call it, is one who is going through it him/herself. Admittedly, those individuals who don't seem to have compassion for the single folk need to get a clue. I once went in to my chiropractor's office and the receptionist asked how I was. I told her I was a bit bummed because something hadn't worked out with someone and I was kind of riding out the discomfort. Without hesitation, she launched into this lengthy explanation about her boyfriend and how everything was extraordinary. Not good. She was so wrapped up in her world that she forgot others might be having a very different experience.

I'll leave this chapter with a question that arose in my therapy that led not only my therapist into laughter but myself additionally. I asked her, rhetorically, "How does one make sense of things not working out if one isn't experiencing any anxiety as a side effect? Is this where religion comes in handy?" I guess that is up to the individual. I say this because I do in fact experience anxiety about the issue of relationships. This can be a useful tool and feeler to explore what is going on. It can also be a real weight-bearing problem in that it can be very counter-productive. I make the comment about religion because I have a girlfriend, Alex, eight years older than I, who relies on her faith and doesn't appear to have the anxiety that I do for example. Each person has to determine what will be most useful in working through a situation that is unpleasant (being single) and look for a way to not let it take over one's life in such a way so that no enjoyment exists.

9

CHECK PLEASE

Men seem to be attracted to women when they appear less threatening and less established. For example, men may pursue women who are waitresses or students and women who are less settled more frequently than well-established women. Men often appear intimidated by powerful career oriented, independent women. In addition, men are wary of women who are potentially after their money and/or have the expectation of "being taken care of." This is understandable. Ideally, it seems that a balance needs to be found between valuing and promoting independence and where tradition lies. All too often men respond negatively when the women are independent, live on their own, have a career, and are content. I think that is why women with condos and cats get such a bad rap. I mean, these women are successful enough to buy their own property, yet they are shunned.

Money and success can work for and against people who date. I recently saw an old friend of mine, Allison, who comes from a lot of money. She told me that her older sister owns her own flat in San Francisco and that once men see her place they either feel extremely threatened or they are attracted, thinking she could be a sugar mama of sorts. This seems to happen with both of them. To be a woman in her thirties who owns a place in Manhattan (as Allison does) or in San Francisco (as her sister does) is great, but not necessarily for a man who wants to be the masculine provider. I suggested to her that she delay or not bring men to her home. She agreed that she might need to do this.

Money, money, money. Everyone has his or her own philosophy about this issue. There are so many factors that play into the way in which it is handled. Of course, how traditional is the man or woman, how were they raised, how much money do they have, how secure are they in their masculinity and/or femininity and how much is equality an important factor to him/her in the dating arena. These are only some of the questions that should be asked.

So, who should pay? Well, I can only share my opinion and experiences. People can absorb what they wish from what I say. I think the woman should not assume that the man will pay unless the woman is very traditional. I have found that most of the time (and let me say that I've dated a lot of very different people) the man will choose to pay. I think that men do appreciate it when women offer. It is more the principal than anything. The man, then, chooses to usually pay anyway. Time and time again, men have said to me that they like the woman to offer but don't expect the women to pay, at least in the beginning.

I think it is presumptuous to assume that the man will always pay in this day and age when there is such a focus on equal rights between men and women. If equality is so important, why should the man pay? This philosophy of mine may be a bit too progressive for some, but I still feel that one should not assume that the other person will pay. Now, here is a perfect example of how we could apply the aforementioned light exercise. Let's say that you, the reader, feel, as a woman, the man should always pay and you are a traditionalist. You would then place this in your green light section. And, if on the first date he takes your money to apply it to the bill, then you know you will not go out with him again. Isn't that great? The first date can tell a lot of things and cut through a lot of bullshit.

Tyler was a bit weird with money. We were courting and we always ended up splitting the bill. It turns out that the guy was 35, living at home (red light), didn't have his own car because he couldn't decide on what to buy and had actually returned a car he'd bought (two red lights, one yellow). He was also very traditional, a bit machismo, yet wanted everything equal (yellow light). Over time, as we became closer and spent time together, he began to stay over at my house a lot, usually on the weekends. He would eat my food, use my phones, use my computer, and essentially made himself at home. This was not uncomfortable for me necessarily because I felt like being generous. But, here is the dilemma…how is it then equal? It actually took a conversation about my generosity to influence his decision to be more "fair" by paying for more meals. Yuck!!!!! The guy was a penny pincher (red light) and this was difficult for me. I ended it quickly.

So, lastly, this man with whom I shared SIX months of my life gave me a hard time for throwing out a *Ziploc* baggie after I'd used it to carry a sandwich on a picnic we had. I am generally not a wasteful person, but a line has to be drawn as to what is practical versus what is wasteful. He was nuts for being so hung up on this. Sadly, he felt some need to continue to bring this up a number of times when we were processing why "we" weren't working and what we could attribute it to. So much for being "fair."

I want to take this opportunity here to defend Jewish men who are often targeted as being spendthrift. This is not always the case. I dated a Conservative Jewish guy, "Monkey Man," who was very generous and not hung up on this issue. He usually treated me to things and was conscious of what he used while he was at my home. Money was simply never an issue with him.

A related incident makes me chuckle now but really pissed me off when I heard this. Jess and I were at an event in this past year. There were two men and six women out to dinner. No love connection was made by anyone. That was fine for everyone I'm sure. When we arrived, the two men wandered off and ran into a group of other people. My friend and I hung out, talked, and took in the scenery. We decided to walk to get a glass of wine. The two men happened to be en route to the bar area. As we approached the vicinity, one of them says twice, "Here they come." We smiled, proceeded, and then agreed that they must have been referencing us. We immediately wanted to find out what the hell they were talking about.

I initially asked the person who didn't make the comment and he claimed that he had no idea what I was talking about. Jess and I felt this was a bit suspect and opted to ask the man who told him that we were coming. He didn't hesitate. He told us that the other guy said, "I don't want to have to buy them drinks." Crazy. Frustrating. Lame. There was no reason he would have had to and we felt that was pretty shallow. Maybe he was making an assumption about us being gold diggers or opportunists. We let it go and I think were happy that the one man didn't seem to agree with his "tight-wad-like" friend.

Recently, I heard of another funny money story. A friend of mine, Darla, had a date set for a Thursday with a man who she had corresponded with via email. Ironically, she had just met a different man earlier that week and was hooked. She already knew things would go forward with the first guy and knew she had to tell the Thursday guy that she had met the other person. During dinner she broached the subject, to which he replied, "Then, why are we here?" She explained that she felt she didn't want to flake and she thought they could become just friends. What happened when the bill came? She said, "Let's split it." He replied, "Let's" with a smug-like expression. This is a tough one. I don't think there is a "right" way to deal with this one. I think some men who were less resentful would have handled it differently.

I have a sad story to share that touches on the issue of money. After graduate school, I moved into an apartment with Lizbeth. This apartment complex was reminiscent of Melrose Place. There were a number of single people living in it. The first day, while I was schlepping things into the place, one of the men, Greg, offered to assist me. From that point on, we all ended up spending a lot of time hanging out together. After a period of time had passed, he learned of my woeful credit situation. I had a number of credit cards and a bit of debt (after all, who doesn't after graduate school?).

So, here I was, with my first job making about 30K a year, feeling adult, a mere 25 years, and stoked to be living by the beach in this complex surrounded by singles. He asked if he could borrow money, sobbing, explaining he'd gotten a DUI and that he had nowhere else to turn. He explained that I could take a cash advance out on my credit card and that he would make the payments monthly when I got the statements. I vacillated about the loan and ultimately agreed. Big mistake.

I thought that by signing a contract in which his computer and a nice watch were to be used as collateral I'd be safe. Not true. Though he made the first few payments, he soon showed his true colors. He started to pay me late, then forget, then come up with excuses that he didn't have the money. It actually got to the point where he would yell and get defensive and tell me to get off of his back. I think the most painful and frustrating part was that I was privy to how he was spending his money: taking women out, partying excessively, vacationing, and going to Vegas to gamble. In addition, I had kept the loan a secret. I did this in part because he asked me to and because, after some time, I experienced a great amount of guilt and shame.

I realized later, after ultimately sharing my situation with people, that I had a bleeding heart. He was an excellent actor. I felt bad for him, felt it was no skin off my back, and felt I could trust him. Feeling like an adult and making more money than I had ever before, I thought I could handle it. After all, he was my neighbor. I ultimately took him to court, won, received a judgment, and garnished his wages. I received about half of what I'd lent him. I believe in Karma and have no doubt he has it coming to him. I also learned that we all make mistakes of various kinds in our lives. I can't say that I've made many big ones, but I can say that this was my mistake in my younger years and I've forgiven myself for it.

It turns out that he had swindled at least five other women. Each one had been taken for anywhere between 5K and 30K. We all fit the same mold. We were all intelligent, successful, and compassionate. None of us were really gullible. Knowing that I wasn't the only one made me feel better. We all agreed that he was truly an excellent con artist.

When I divulge this experience to men whom I have met or had relationships with, they all have the same types of responses. They are angry, frustrated, feel sad, and bombard me with questions I think in part due to a tendency to want to protect me. They all wonder if my neighbor and I were in a relationship or if we dated one another. Truth be told, we did have a fling. I did actually have an interest in him initially because of his capacity to weasel out of situations and because he was very bright. Ultimately, I did lose all respect and attraction toward him. There was most likely a connection between my initial intrigue and my willingness to lend him money, though I wasn't involved with him when I did lend him the money. The lesson here is to not lend people money unless there is a clear guarantee that you will get it back.

10

FORMS OF CONVERSATION AND COMMUNICATION

Conversation abilities and styles in the dating world vary greatly. I once had a conversation with my girlfriend Jan. She was single at the time and she expressed to me that she had no clue as to how to engage in small talk. This worried her because small talk is so important in the dating world. I was at a loss and could suggest nothing. I realized that engaging in casual chitchat can be very difficult. I think people who are accustomed to having intense or intellectual conversations wrestle with small talk. But, one might say that it is imperative in the early stages of dating to engage in small talk as a means of getting to know someone slowly but surely. Jan must have overcome her inability to chitchat, because she entered the area of pharmaceutical sales and was required to engage in a tremendous amount of small talk and schmoozing. She also met a great man, got engaged, and is now married.

The question of how to flirt also has come up periodically with my friends. Flirting reflects a person's communication style. My belief is that, for some, flirting is inherent and natural. Some just have the flirting bug in them and don't have to make any effort to succeed. Others, on the other hand, tend to have to make a conscious effort to attract anyone by flirting. Then, there are the last few who are not flirts and don't necessarily need or care to make any effort to flirt in order to meet people.

For anyone who needs specific tips as to flirting and how to go about it, I do have a couple of suggestions. One is to actually smile. It has been my experience that smiling makes a person seem approachable and interested. This is sort of a simple fact yet it is forgotten. In addition, being conscious of body language is important. There are, for example, different ways of hugging people. There is the long hug, the pat on the back hug, the tight embrace hug, the reach around and grab your booty hug, and I'm sure others. There is a book, *Signals*, which I read years ago that I believe has a lot of great material on the topic of communication, of which flirting is a form.

One of my own pet peeves regarding communication style that I have developed over the years is people who repeat themselves over and over. The person you know as "the repeater." I have had many experiences in which a man and I will have the same conversation and I am the only one who knows we already had this conversation. Honestly, no one needs to hear the same thing over and over. This becomes taxing and quite annoying after a while. My philosophy as to why men become repeaters is that some men need to tell their stories repeatedly in order to work through issues. Also, I think they ask questions repeatedly because they simply are not listening for the answers. Men who ask the same question over and over become incredibly frustrating ALSO. Ultimately, one starts to feel that there is no reason to actually say a damn thing because the guy isn't listening.

Recently, I dated a man who was a genuine repeater. He asked me three different questions more than once and denied that he had already asked me these questions. I responded jokingly, saying, "That must have been someone else you asked." I was frustrated and annoyed. Not to be ball-buster-like, but, my God, pay attention!!!! I am aware that not everyone has the same type of steel-trap memory. However, when two people are courting, I think they should make it a priority to remember the questions and answers that have been posed. This is a way in which I think men can impress women and vice versa (though it might scare a man a little bit when a woman remembers everything) and people should be cognizant of this.

It should also go without saying that one should say what they mean and mean what they say. It seems all too often, especially in the dating arena, that people just say completely different things than what they feel or think. It starts to make one wonder what they can believe and what they should believe. My thinking about this is that it is hard to be both direct and honest. But, as painful as it may be in anticipation or in the moment, there is a sense of freedom and relief in the long run.

In speaking to this point also, there is the idea of thinkers versus doers. There have been so many times in which I was privy to (whether it be my own or a friend's) situations when the man has demonstrated a thought about something and has indicated he plans to do something with that thought, yet no action occurs. For example, "We should do this." Or "We should go there." Or, "When is your birthday?" It's something I think people need to be both more conscious of (those who say it) and more skeptical of (those who hear it). It is a difference to be with a doer rather than a thinker. Is a thinker a green, yellow, or red light for you?

11

TO CALL OR NOT TO CALL

In the dating world there are phone etiquette rules. Many people say women should not call a man first, but should let the man do so. Personally, my belief is that the timing of the call and who should call *really* depends on the people and the situation. What is interesting is that the phone can be used as a tool to both avoid and skirt issues and as a method to really corner someone. Leaving messages on someone's phone can sometimes be a safety mechanism in that both people avoid having to directly have a scary, hurtful or frustrating conversation. Men underestimate the phone in this arena. For example, I recently met someone and we went on a date. I knew I didn't like him but he liked me. I didn't want to blow him off or not call so I called when I knew he would be at work and left him a message saying thanks but I just didn't think we clicked. I cannot begin to tell you how many times I have done this. Another key to gently rejecting someone is to make it about yourself rather than the other person. It is important to use sentences with "I" and "me" rather than "you." Many a time I have been thanked for doing this. Both people end up feeling good despite the circumstances and they both can move on without anxiety.

How to take advantage of phone calling options is also important to single people. My friend close friend Jack told me about an interesting experience using the convenient, but scary *69 feature on his phone. He had been seriously involved with a woman who was back home while he was working for a summer in a different state. He said that he suspected her of cheating on him during their time apart, but he didn't have any evidence of her infidelity. Conveniently, she called him at his work once but he wasn't available. Instead of waiting for her to call again, he *69'd her just a few minutes later to see if she was calling from a different place. Being quite slick about it, he asked my sister to call, pretend she was someone else, and ask to speak with his girlfriend. What happened? You guessed it. A man answered, Jack's girlfriend was there, and she was caught! I wonder what would've happened without that *69 feature.

Caller ID can be a single person's best friend. If a man or woman calls repeatedly without leaving a message, you can bust them with caller ID. If you want to avoid their call and do not want to talk to them you can do so by using caller ID, and you don't have to stop answering your phone for days at a time.

Leaving messages on a pager, voice mail, or work number can make it easier to tell someone the difficult news that you aren't interested in them. If you don't want to have a confrontation or conflict, but you want to be respectful enough of the other person to let them know you're not interested in dating, leave a message. My philosophy is that there is no reason why people shouldn't at least let the other person know if they are uninterested. I mean, they don't have to talk to the person, but at least call and let them know so they aren't left hanging. I understand that people don't want to hurt another person's feelings and that many men and women would rather just blow the person off or avoid their calls and not deal with it. But, most people agree that rather than blowing someone off, it is better to call and leave a message when you know the individual isn't home.

I have had a few dates with men who failed to ever directly tell me a) that they weren't interested and b) why they weren't. I met a man at a bar one time and we went out a couple of times and had a great time. He actually wasn't really my type but I was attracted to him. We had plans to hang out again with no set time. I didn't hear from him for a while and felt confused because we seemed to get along well. I thought, that's fine, no big deal, but don't leave me hanging. So, I called him at work when I knew he wouldn't be there and left a message inquiring about where he stood, very casual, no pressure. In the message I left my voicemail so that he wouldn't have to talk with me directly if he didn't want to. He still didn't call. I guess one can't expect everyone to use voicemail in this way, but I sure recommend it.

I think what it comes down to is it sucks when someone doesn't call back and the other person is left wondering why. My suggestion is to call. I have been in a couple of situations in which I called a guy out of respect to let them know it wasn't working for me. In every instance, he has been thankful and appreciative and it has left me feeling good and relieved. Try it.

12

WAYS TO MEET PEOPLE

Great restaurants may be one site for dating, but connections can occur anywhere. I now believe in the idea that people actually meet at gas stations, grocery stores, and the bank. Once, I was filling my car with gas and this man walked up to me. He wasn't my type, but he was cute. He asked if I was interested in purchasing one of those coupon books for various services at the shop. I told him that I wasn't interested but he persisted and continued to converse with me. He had an accent (a lot of people seem to find accents very sexy and this can be intriguing) and I learned he was from Scotland. Needless to say, I was quite intrigued and excited. He was very kind and extremely complimentary. We chatted a bit and he insisted I take his number and call if I wanted to play.

Ironically, I wasn't looking particularly good that day and never would have expected something like this to happen. I did end up calling him and we dated off and on for a few months. He was here in the states temporarily, making extra money from selling the coupons. He also taught soccer to kids and was a very happy person. I think I learned a few lessons from this that I feel are worth sharing: 1. You don't always have to look your best for something to manifest. 2. You shouldn't judge someone for what they do right away because you have no idea what is going on with them. 3. You really *can* meet someone at a gas station.

The Scottish guy story reminds me of an *Ally McBeal* episode in which a man behind the coffee bar counter hit on her. She thought he was cute and nice but wouldn't go out with him because of what he did, or her perception of what he did. It turns out he was the owner and wanted to experience being on the other side, just as a regular guy. He was not only the owner of this but was a top-level executive type with a lot of money. It just goes to show you that being shallow can bite you in the ass. Scottish guy and I did date for a bit, stopped, and then I ran into him not once, but twice, months later. These run-ins are a real mixed bag. We rekindled briefly but our differences were too great.

Meeting people when it's unplanned, uncalculated, and unexpected is I think by far the best possible scenario.

There is also speed dating. Either the men sit at a specified table while the women rotate or vice versa. There is usually a set age group and a facilitator who times the hopeful non-mundane encounters. These encounters are usually between 3 and 8 minutes and one meets up to 25 people. Basically, it is a number of mini-dates. The beauty of it is that there are no exchanges of phone numbers or anything throughout the entire evening and not quite enough time to feel horribly anxious or uncomfortable if you don't particularly like the other person. When all is said and done, you hand in a paper in which you've circled names of individuals with whom you'd like to have further conversation. Within a couple of days, you receive information about whether you have a match with those individuals. It almost seems the most ideal for someone like me. It's fast, no pressure, you can figure things out quickly and then it's over. It's good for someone who has the confidence that they can size someone up quickly. I have tried it and it has been fun and much easier for my personality type than other methods. As much as this has been a positive experience overall, I think I've decided to take a break from planned encounters for a while and rely on the unexpected ones.

There are always: religious affiliations; work conventions and conferences; banks (this has yet to happen to me); gas stations (I can say this has happened to me); grocery stores; home depot and random street encounters. I have three great stories of different women friends of mine who have met people in this fashion, lending to some hope.

Jess was wandering the aisles of a grocery store and met a man. They began talking and seemed to clique. She then became a bit nervous, saw him a couple of other times and was indeed tempted to ask him out. She, at the time, felt it was more his responsibility and thus didn't do anything. However, it put a smile on her face and we did get a kick out of it.

An even better story is that Jen met someone at Home Depot. This guy said to her, while looking at a rose bush, "When the rose gets bigger, could I give you my number and have you page me?" She chuckled and opted not to because she knew he wasn't for her. She did feel good and he, too, left her with a smile on her face, recharging her with some needed hope.

My girlfriend, Megan, was walking, smiling, along the streets of Pasadena. She sees a group of men just hanging out and says hello to one of them. He returns the hello and he catches up with her. They chat a little and he wishes her a good night. About a week later she's back in Pasadena and they run into each other at a bar. They are both shocked and believe this was some sort of destiny situation.

They exchange numbers and end up hanging out one night. This speaks to the vast amount of possibilities that can occur when meeting someone. You just never know!

13

STORIES OF SINGLE EVENTS

The following are stories gathered from a variety of women, including myself, about their experiences looking for Mr. Right at a singles event. Both men and women can find these events frustrating. Men often complain that they dramatically outnumber the women. No one can be certain that a singles event will include an equal number of men and women.

Sasha and I learned about an organization catering to people with masters and doctorate degrees, named Advanced Degrees. They host a variety of events at different places. We researched it, spoke with a representative and decided to drive just short of an hour to branch out with what we thought would be bright people with whom we might have a few things in common. Well, something quite different happened. When we arrived, looking and feeling good, we saw very few. We reassured one another and decided to play a game of pool, all the while knowing we had put a lot of energy into this and that patience and an open mind were of utmost importance. As time went on, we began to see a theme. Much to our surprise, each individual arriving was no less than twice our age! We were shocked, dumbfounded, and ultimately pretty frustrated. We approached the promoter and explained our concern and, at that time, he did indicate we might in fact be on the "younger side." Thanks to my assertive friend, our money was refunded and we left in hysterics.

The whole night included one calamity after another. We were in a town far from home, all dressed up and nowhere to go, driving along. To add to the crazy making evening, we both had allergies, our feet were incredibly sore and my contact fell out while driving back to Los Angeles. I had to hold the contact in my mouth while driving for 45 minutes. I also managed to spit a large mouthful of water on my windshield because we were laughing so hard. Lesson: make sure that you are aware of all definitions of a word used in the name of a singles club. "Advanced" in age was more like it.

Joy and I went to a Comedy Singles event about a year later. We had heard about this event in which a person hosts a comedian at his/her house and people eat appetizers, drink wine, and socialize. After speaking with the comedian and being reassured that this was a very casual, fun, and interesting event (and age appropriate, we were reassured) we decided to go.

Prior to attending, we decided to get a drink, have a little grub, and review various signs and hand gestures that would cover all the possible outcomes the evening could hold: Joy meets someone she is interested in whereas I want to leave, me meeting someone interesting and Joy wanting to leave, she needing to be rescued, me needing to be rescued, both of us wanting to leave, and of course, the most hopeful, both of us wanting to stay because we'd both found someone we were interested in. I am certain we spent at least an hour on all of these gestures. It was so funny that we were expending such a great deal of time on an unforeseeable scenario. The experience in and of itself was enjoyable and entertaining to say the least. A fly on the wall would've had quite a field day listening to all of the potential situations and solutions we were able to come up with.

We arrived, feeling a bit too young, and immediately went for the wine, working our way through the crowd. As we approached the table we realized there was a very large selection of wine. We were pleased. Discussing what wine to choose, a man hovered over, and almost desperately, smiled and begged to pour both of us a glass. It was at that moment we exchanged glances and knew we had to depart. We smiled, thanked the nice fellow, took a couple of sips of the wine, and walked out. We went to the car and laughed aloud at the fact that we had expended such great energy on our plan as to how to handle all of the possibilities. Little did we know our endeavor would last a mere five minutes.

Jess encouraged me to go with her to a Jewish Shabbat dinner. The dinner was to cater to singles and include food, drinks, the service, and mingling. Because I did not grow up in a religious home, I had never been to a Shabbat dinner. I thought, if anything, I could get something out of this and get in touch a bit more with my cultural background. On the other hand, I felt a bit awkward because this wasn't my type of gig.

We were dressed to the hilt, feeling good, and expectation free, having learned from previous singles events not to hope for too much. We scoped out the place, and, upon time to sit, decided to try to find a table with reasonably attractive men. We couldn't seem to find one, but finally came across a table with a nice looking woman who said, "hello," introduced herself as Darla, and asked us to sit down near her. Upon further discussion it turned out that she had come to the event with two close male friends, both whom were single and wanting to sit near some "cute women." She felt we fit the bill. We both sat down, Jess next to an empty chair, and I on her other side, with an empty chair next to me. It wasn't more than two minutes later that a man asked if the seat next to me was available. I told him it was. This was the first mistake. He then began to strike up a conversation and out of the corner of my eye I noticed the other two men talking with Darla and Jess. And, there I was, stuck, and no place to go.

Essentially I did not want to talk with this needy man with whom I had nothing in common. I would have rather conversed with someone more attractive and intriguing. And, I wanted to enjoy the Shabbat with Jess. This guy was desperate to connect with someone. He was suffocating me. I literally had to turn my back on him. He couldn't read my body language when I just stared ahead and ignored everything he said. Admittedly, I did feel a bit guilty.

It just so turned out that the other men were interested in us, and Darla turned out to be a blast. We had a great time talking and hanging out with her afterwards. When we asked more about the men, in the bathroom of course, we realized that the guys were not men we would connect with. Why else was she just friends with them? Lesson #1: Make sure you don't leave an open seat next to you at an event where you have not seen anyone you are attracted to. Lesson #2: Always know that sometimes you may make a great woman friend out of a single's event, and be open to it.

Sasha and I went to an orientation for an organization catering to singles with a focus on events, entertainment, and physical activities (biking, boating, skiing, etc.). We were excited about the possibilities and thought we would investigate. As we arrived, a woman greeted us. We were both struck by her nasal tone, her 80's attire, her lisp, and her incredibly cheery disposition. She was actually a very pleasant and friendly woman with a lot of spunk, which made her perfect for leading an event such as this.

Despite her positive qualities, however, we couldn't help but be frustrated. The woman discussed not having friends when she first came to L.A. and that, when she joined this organization, she was able to meet people easily. This seemed to make logical sense and seemed to have worked for her. However, the way in which she presented herself and her experience left the impression that the perks of joining the group were not for us. The group constituted an opportunity to make friends for newcomers to L.A. or for people with limited social skills and/ or involvement in extracurricular activities.

We also couldn't help but wonder, if this was ideally a forum in which to meet other singles in which to pursue a relationship, why was she, after three years, still single? The icing on the cake was that, out of about a dozen people at the orientation, only two were men. Of course, the facilitator said this was atypical. It was at that point that Sasha and I exchanged glances reflecting that frustrating, it's Murphy's Law, look. The whole evening turned out to be a bust. From the beginning we could not get past this woman's attire. She essentially looked like she had never left the 1980's. She had the white stirrup stretch pants, big hair sprayed hair with pink lipstick and long brightly painted nails. This group was specifically for sports minded singles; we wondered how she could actually participate in sports with those monstrosities on her hands. We decided not to return.

In search of that special opportunity or event, a couple of single girlfriends and I took a wine tasting class. This seemed to be a win-win situation in that we would at least learn something and be able to drink some good wine. If we connected with someone, there would be an added bonus. Besides, we were together.

We looked for some seats, and, again, in the danger zone, left were seats next to, you guessed it, a SLM! He was pleasant, sweet, and desperate for making that connection. Fortunately, my friend who had a bit more patience than I sat next to him and interacted periodically with him without feeling too sad for him. Here is the kicker…we were yelled at and ostracized because we laughed and talked too much. Well, sorry for having a good time.

My sense was that the leader of the course needed to feel in control and that he didn't feel central enough. We were the focus of attention, making jokes, laughing and going on. He actually threatened to ask us to leave. The evening brought all of us back to those instances that happen so frequently throughout school in which you begin laughing when you're not supposed to which only makes you laugh even more…you try to contain yourself and you just can't. It was so funny. There were no men we connected with, but we got a great buzz!

My friend Hal had a Singles party with about seventy people. I brought three women friends and a man I know from work. He brought with him three other men. Of course, what would have been ideal would have been that one of the six of us might have connected with another one. I guess that would have been too simple. What was great about this particular party, however, was that Hal only invited single people. The party was interesting in that it was unlike the bar scene in which you don't know who is single or who is looking for love, for a lay, to flirt, to cheat, or to be a wingman. At this party everyone knew everyone was single. Of course, how do you break the ice? There were no nametags. What Hal did do was place a number of various sized screws and bolts in a bucket and had a friend pass around the screws to the men and the bolts to the women. The plan was for people to find their match. The sexual undertone added to the experience, of course. As far as I know, the only person who was successful in a date was Hal himself. I can't say I didn't have fun though. I thought the singles party concept was an awesome idea.

A number of friends have told me about their experiences in Club Med. There are places which are not only singles-focused, but also have a sex theme. If you are interested in an adventure in which anything goes, I highly suggest the hedonism-style Club Med getaways. I will say that those friends of mine who have gone have had a great time, enjoyed meeting people and shtuping others, and essentially received some serious ego stroking. I admit, I do like to have my ego stroked. I guess my hope is that I'll have my ego stroked by someone whose salary doesn't come from getting into peoples pants.

I earlier mentioned my trip to Mexico with Eve. This was not a Club Med, but rather an all-inclusive trip with other individuals from the Los Angeles area. Though it was not specific to singles, I was told that a number of singles would be there. I tried to keep a positive attitude about this situation, seeing as I'd learned how disconcerting having expectations (great expectations, for that matter) can be. So, at the least, we enjoyed gorging ourselves with authentic food, drinking, and relaxing, and soaking up the sun. Well, it is no wonder that I'd just decided to write this book just prior to our trip. A variety of pertinent information occurred, such that I felt it useful to touch on.

First, I did not meet my future husband but I did gain several insights as to how confusing the dating scene is and how damaging mixed messages can be. Essentially, a man there pursued me in an incredibly aloof fashion. As strange as that may seem, he was flirtatious and wanted to hang out and fool around, yet this was extremely intermittent. It was quite a confusing dynamic. Second, I learned that beach based aquatic vacations are not for everyone. The friend I went with said, after the trip was over, "I don't think this is the type of vacation I should be taking, seeing as I don't like to get my face wet." Third, I was stalked by a man who had a lot of issues and wasn't, again, able to read signs of disinterest. Here I'm referring to the stalker. Fourth, I ended up spending a great deal of time with fellow single men who were going through struggles similar to ours. This was both interesting and useful because we could all empathize with one another, while it was irritating because it felt annoying to hear some of their specific commentary that validated, unbeknownst to them, a lot of what my women friends and I discuss. Fifth, Eve and I were, on average, eight years younger than most of the people there. The least bit refreshing, provoking concern was that we may in fact be in the same situation as those on the trip come eight years from now. Lastly, I had a realization of what <u>not</u> to do after I end a relationship. Specifically, I realized that it can be detrimental to be around people whose main source of connecting with one another is to discuss woes about male and female dynamics and what isn't working. This can feed into the sadness or anxiety one may have about a break up. On the contrary, if one is looking for an ego boost or a distraction of some sort, this can be a great venue for such an experience. So, singles trips can be rewarding while not always the perfect fit for everybody.

Benefits for charities often draw those looking for love. I did meet a man at such an event. This particular event, we were told, was to be quite large and attended by a number of single people. Another added plus to most benefits is that the cost is tax deductible. It turned out that Jess knew other people who were going and we ended up eating out in a group of two men and six women before the event. You might have guessed that ALL eight, yes ALL eight were single. We talked, as I typically do, about dating, blind dates, Internet dates, and the like…it was interesting, but also felt as if it were the SAME old crap that is sadly too often the focus of conversation whenever people are single. I felt as if I was back in Mexico.

The one plus of the evening was that I was actually curious about and interested in one of the men, Shane. When he described what he looks for in a woman, I felt like saying, "Wait! That's me, that's me!!!!!!" I used my better judgment and refrained from shouting this out. What I did do, the following day, was ask Jess to ask her friend for his email so that I could drop him a line. One additional aspect of the story is that he had dated Jess's friend a few times. He was not interested in her any longer, but she was still interested in him. Oh, the torment of unrequited love! So, I had to be sensitive and careful, but felt, "You only live once…you've got to give it a try." So, I emailed him and we did date off and on for a while.

At this time I was starting a sports club, not singles specific, for people to get together monthly and play different sports, and I used this as a segue into the email. I asked Shane if he would be interested in going to coffee or for a drink and informed him of the group. Turns out, knowing many commonalities we had, we were members of the same gym and we ran into each other there after I'd sent him the email but he'd not yet read it. What are the chances of us running into each other? He said yes to both the following day. We met a couple of days later at a bar. I was so excited and nervous, I had a stiff drink before I met him. When I arrived, he wasn't there. So, I looked around for a place to sit and chose an area a bit elevated from the rest of the bar, in plain view of the entrance. I ordered a drink. I then decided I wasn't comfortable and opted to move else-where. I found a seat near the bar area and waited, uncomfortably, for about 5 minutes. I then decided to move again, all the while chuckling to myself, think-ing anyone who is watching (and I was convinced and paranoid that everyone was) must think I'm a nut case. I found a seat at a table and waited another few minutes. He finally arrived and asked if I wouldn't mind moving to the original seat I'd picked, of course. I laughed and agreed.

We seemed to have a great deal in common. This was actually quite refreshing because I typically don't feel this way. I was impressed because he had been in therapy, he was driven intellectually and occupationally, he seemed sensitive, open, curious, and appreciated my sense of humor. We also seemed to share experiences and views of dating and it's difficulties. He definitely received a lot of "points" that night. I then told him I'd be interested in hanging out again if he did. He smiled.

We walked to the car and he gave me a kiss goodnight. There was no discus-sion of further meeting, but I knew I'd hear from him again. Something was sus-pect though. We spoke the next week and ultimately saw one another when I arranged the first sports gathering. I hadn't felt this compatible with someone in quite some time so I was excited. Another kiss goodbye. I then didn't hear from him for some time and had a dilemma. I didn't know if I should call or if he would or what to do. Fortunately, I had an excuse. I needed a date for a reception the following week. I called and invited him and he said yes. We went and had a great time and kissed some more at the end.

Now, one would think all things point to "go" given the kissing and sequence of events. For me, there were a ton of green lights and my sense was that there were a number of green lights for him. When we spoke on the phone, we laughed, and could be serious would talk for hours at a time. What I couldn't understand was why he wasn't pursuing me more (after all, we'd not really had an official date and we'd only seen each other about every two weeks). I even asked what he thought of dating and me I'd shared with him that I was getting mixed messages. I was actually convinced that he was uncertain about me because he hadn't yet seen me dressed up in a sexy outfit. I was pleased when I'd had the opportunity to dress up for the reception so that he could see me this way. He actually complimented me a number of times. Should this much thought be going into this though, I'd thought to myself?

When I asked him how he felt about dating, he exclaimed, "I hate it, it feels like research, I feel this is what I have to do because that's what everyone our age is doing, and it's a pain and if I had more patience and energy I'd date every night." I was left thinking, shit, this doesn't help me any because I don't know what he's doing with me. And, I'm thinking, if you're so picky (as am I) and don't like dating, then why don't you hang out with me a bit more and see where this is going. Of course, I kept these thoughts to myself, as difficult as it was. I also knew, based on his sharing of previous dating scenarios, that if he isn't interested in someone, he is direct and tells them so. He hadn't told me as much.

There are a number of rules in the dating world, some offered by women, some by men. By and large, most people believe that the men should pursue and that if the man is interested he will in his own time frame. I guess I didn't feel as though I wanted to wonder for that long. How long was his time frame? I also didn't feel that remaining just friends would have been practical or healthy, seeing as I had an already active social life. And, judging as to how things went with Shane, I wagered that I would have only become more and more fond of him, all the while becoming more and more frustrated because his light wasn't "on" to have a relationship. I consulted with friends and everyone had a different take, influenced by their own experiences, age, and gender, of course. Ultimately, knowing that this wasn't comfortable for me not having heard from him in some time, I called and asked him about it. It turned out he was not really interested in developing something with someone at that point. His head was focused on work and another Master's degree. We discussed it and acknowledged it wasn't going to happen for us at that time and said a cordial goodbye.

After a month or two, I emailed him to let him know I'd be interested in hanging out as we were and that I was cool with not being anything more. He responded with a resounding yes and we made plans for the upcoming weekend. He actually took me out and we had a good time. You just never know what may come out of trying different approaches to difficult dating scenarios. It's now been a couple of years since our meeting and we've developed a wonderful close friendship.

I think it is pertinent here to mention something quite entertaining about all of this. I had invited Darla to the sporting event at the beach. After I'd eaten lunch with Shane before the event, he had gone off on his own for a bit, while I went to meet the people at the beach. We talked and caught up a bit. She tells me that she'd been on a date a couple of days prior and that it wasn't a match. She then goes on to describe that they were then discussing the upcoming weekend and that it turns out that they were both going to the sporting event. Her date was with Shane! Talk about a small world.

Then, to top it off, remembering my reference to the Mexico trip and "stalker drunk"…there we are gathering together readying for the game and up comes

Darla's friend…the stalker! This was just too weird, a strange day after all. She thought I must hate her but we laughed about it. It all turned out okay. The odd part was that Shane hadn't told me about Darla when we were at lunch. He indicated later that it didn't seem like a big deal to him. We all ended up playing the game (Darla, the stalker, Shane, and I) had a great time!

14

LONG DISTANCE DATING

Long distance dating can be fun, intriguing, scary, frustrating, *and* "safe." It can be a form of mental masturbation, it can be masochistic, it can be a way of avoiding a commitment, and it can be a source of intense highs and lows. Long distance dating can be a distraction, and it can be the beginning of either an end or a wonderful love relationship.

There are a variety of experiences I can reference, some of my own, some of others I know. The one I hold close to my heart was a relationship I had a few years back. I dated a man, Joe, for about two months shortly after college. He was visiting from Montana and living in my college town during this time. We had some fun but didn't really connect. There was an inevitable end in that he was moving back home at the end of summer and in that we were dissimilar in some fundamental ways. We didn't talk for a couple of years. I then heard from him in my last year of graduate school and we reformed a friendship that blossomed over the phone; he remained in Montana and I in California.

We decided that it would be fun for me to visit at some point. With my new job and benefits for the first time in my life, we made plans for me to visit him in Montana. We had an incredible time. We connected, laughed, talked and talked…it felt as if we had been life long friends. It was that level of comfort you don't find with just anyone. Interestingly, neither of us expected it to go as well as it did and we had also, over the four years of being apart, become more similar in our ways.

So, what to do next? What ensued was a five-month relationship of frequent phone calls and visiting one another about once a month. I visited him two times, he visited me, we met half way one time, and we went to Greece together. It had just so happened that his parents were taking an annual trip to a small island in Greece and were planning to take him along. I was invited. How could I have refused? A few things happened on this trip. First, it is very difficult to spend any length of time with someone on vacation when there is no escape and I, not for one minute, felt the least bit sick of him. How refreshing! Second, I think when two people are together in a romantic situation, it can feel closer (sometimes this is reality and sometimes it is delusional). I felt genuinely closer to him. So much so that I felt that I was falling in love. How wonderful! How scary! How worrisome! How frustrating! It took every effort on my part to stay in the moment. Third, his parents were great. I felt very at ease with them, as they appeared to with me. It was a wonderful foursome on this trip. And the trip was truly the best vacation I had: romantic, wonderful, blissful, and all together phenomenal.

You can imagine that parting ways was challenging to say the least. The following months consisted of the aforementioned closeness and confusion. Ultimately, I ended the relationship because of the distance and because I felt he was not interested in a relationship that potentially involved long term commitment. This was a devastating experience, but I know it was ultimately the best thing I could have done. Now he lives closer to me than Montana because of his work, and we are friends who correspond periodically. I don't think I would have traded this long distance relationship for anything. I at least had an opportunity to feel what it is like, as an adult in my twenties, to be truly in love with someone and to feel a sincere connection.

A funny anecdote occurred a few years later when he came to visit. It must've been about 3 years since we'd seen each other and he was newly out of a relationship. We decided he'd sleep in my bed and basically he asked, "Can I see your boobs?" He'd been a fan. Essentially, there was this whole awkwardness in the negotiation. Do I show him, and if so, how. It was hysterical…we didn't take it any further than that but got a laugh about the little episode.

A little different from this situation of mine is one that my Korean friend, Eve, encountered. In her case I think it was about being attracted to the unavailable man, the man who she couldn't have a commitment with, a man who was safe for that very reason. She met him one night, when we were out dancing, and they had a blast together. He was visiting the U.S. from Norway with friends, doing the U.S. summer tour. He invited her back to his hotel. They spent the night together and had an awesome time.

What transpired afterward was an intense cyberspace relationship via emails. They wrote each other daily for a number of months. Eventually they confessed their love to one another. This actually became quite worrisome seeing as she had only spent one night with him. She did come to her senses after some time had passed and finally confronted the issue. They spoke and agreed to stop the long distance communication. Some people, like Eve in this instance, feel safer and experience a sense of freedom choosing and cultivating relationships that they know won't work out.

I often wonder about long distance dating because it seems that I frequently meet someone when I am traveling. I don't know why this happens. I genuinely am not looking to meet men while I am away from home. Could it be commitment issues, funny luck, appeal on the man's part, a sense of freedom, or just pure coincidences. I don't believe in coincidences. I think I meet men easily when I am not in Los Angeles because men who are not from L.A. are less jaded than Angeleno men.

One instance in particular that stands out occurred about five years ago when I was visiting friends in northern California. I was at a bar with three friends and met a group of four men. How perfect. The long and the short of it was that one of the men, Jami, paid me a number of compliments and made a move on me. He was kind, sincere, and drunk. We had to leave but he insisted, when we were leaving, that if I wasn't willing to hang out with him that he must have my number. I gave it to him, and he gave me his.

We ended up speaking a lot on the phone over the next few weeks. He paid me a visit and we had fun. I then had a trip planned to Hawaii with a girlfriend of mine and it happened to be through his airline. We arranged it so that I could see him upon my return. We spend a wonderful night together. What seemed then to happen was reality set in. We lived six hours apart via plane (red light); he had a two-year-old son from a previous marriage (yellow light) and was a complete workaholic (red light). The connection dwindled; it was not meant to be.

I also met someone one on the Hawaii trip (this was a good year). He was a real sweetheart, from Portland, Oregon, and a ripe old age of 21! My gosh! Anyway, my friend and I were dancing and met up with these three guys; we knew they were young chickens and they happened to be staying near our hotel. Because we met on the second to last night, on the last night I was left with that moral dilemma of what to do. After much contemplation, my girlfriend and I agreed that I should go for it and enjoy spending time with this young chap. So, I did.

We went and had a couple of beers and ultimately planted ourselves on the beach. The beaches in Hawaii are so romantic. After that trip, I decided that I wouldn't return without a mate because it is too romantic to be enjoyed alone or with a friend. We spent the night on the beach until 5:00 in the morning. No sex. Just sweetness, making out, and getting to know one another. He was so sensitive and sad when we had to part ways. Again, what to do? We ended up writing one another and talking on the phone a few times, and then just stopped the communication. A much younger guy, who lived in Portland, having just graduated from college, was again not the most practical for me.

Around this time period I must have been on a role because I, on yet another trip up north to Chico, met another man. I was hanging out in my girlfriend Delia's bar and we were sitting there shooting the shit. A good-looking, rustic Mountain-man like (remember the reference) walks in with a chocolate lab. Well, here we have a chick magnet. 2 for 2.

We chatted and discussed our lives with Delia and our other friend, Meliss. I learned he was a crop duster pilot. Never heard of this before. The variety of occupations that are out there always fascinates me. You just never know whom you're talking to. I think this is yet another way in which L.A. is so different.

Anyway, we had to leave, and I had a little buzz going on (this always seems to make things both easier and more difficult). He walked us out and laid a nice long wet one on me. He had these sparkling blue eyes and such soft lips. I was beside myself. We agreed we'd talk at some point (he did live in California after all, and he was older, of course). We did talk once on the phone and I realized why he was a crop duster pilot and why he wasn't for me. I didn't feel at all intellectually stimulated by our discussion and I told him, tactfully, that I wasn't interested. We didn't talk again. I did wonder around this time period if I was meant to live up north. I mean, who wouldn't?

A few years back I didn't have set plans for New Years Eve. I was contemplating what to do and had a couple of options. At the last minute I decided to join a friend of mine for dinner, drinks and a huge party. I met up with him at his house where a bunch of people had gathered. Most people there were coupled up but there were a few single people there. I met one of the adorable guys I'd ever seen that night. He was sweet, kind, sexy, intelligent, and a TWIN! I have always had a fondness for twins.

I had, as always, my little mental "checklist" of qualities I like and dislike in a man. The twin, Tony (from Big Bear), was scoring a lot of points throughout the evening. Essentially, we were flirting a little bit and separated ourselves from the group. We danced that night and had a great time. The party was a bit odd and *chichi*, at a big hotel, very Hollywood (which he and I both felt pretty uncomfortable about). As we all left and determined who was going whom, I exclaimed, "Well, Tony is going with me." The funny thing is that I had made the very same comment with Mark (the instructor) when we'd all gone dancing and the same question was posed.

I know such proclamations are very bold, but heck, you only live once (maybe). So, he agreed and said he would need a toothbrush. We went off on our own and he came over. We talked, snuggled, made out, and finally fell asleep. We hung out the next day in bed all day long, and on the couch, watched football, napped, fooled around, and ate. It was awesome. No sex. He wasn't comfortable sleeping together. This only endeared him to me more.

The next day I drove him back to his car. The sad part was that he lived in Big Bear, California. My thinking was that I had made some progress in that he lived only two hours away as opposed to eight or more. We continued to speak regularly on the phone and made plans to hang out. He invited me to visit him in Big Bear. Off I went. It was absolutely gorgeous, snow falling and all. We hung out for hours, dining and drinking, finishing the night off in his hot tub. I'd never had the pleasure of doing that in the snow. It was cute, I'd forgotten a suit (not intentionally, I swear) and he let me wear a pair of his trunks. We didn't even fool around at all. He has a very high level of respect for women and treated me in that fashion. He even assured me, "I don't want you to think I just invited you up here to get laid."

The following day, we ate breakfast and hiked around and ran some errands. My plan had been to leave in the afternoon and that didn't happen. I just couldn't get myself to leave. I did eventually depart at about 10:00 or 11:00 P.M. and felt elated, sad, and anxious all at once. I figured he was a real mench and I dug him totally. We talked a few more times but ultimately it dwindled. I was grateful to my friend for inviting me out that night and I had a couple of really nice days with a great guy.

I must have learned my lesson about the long distance dating issue because, as I sit here, writing this book, I just met someone out of town whom I am not going to pursue things with. Not only does he live in San Diego (where I did live for graduate school), but he's also a mere twenty-three. Funny, I don't know what it is this year with these younger guys. Though, I am convinced that on a certain level, they are less jaded and real potentials. I've yet to meet someone significantly younger, however, who lives locally and can prove my theory.

I had gone dancing with a girlfriend, Jen, and we were having a blast. This guy, fairly short, about my height, started dancing with me. He was pretty cute and not such a bad dancer (now, I've mentioned the dancing turn-on). We danced a lot and then he wanted to talk. Sometimes it is a real pain in the ass to have a conversation in a horrendously loud venue such as a massive dance club, but I persevered. He was asking me the normal stuff and just getting to know a little bit about me.

At some point we discussed our ages. He didn't appear to feel any threat or disappointment about my age or the fact that I lived one hundred miles away. He asked me, "would you even date me then?" I said to him, "What's the point? I mean, you live here, I live in L.A., I'm 30, you're 23, I'm looking for something serious. Don't you just want to get laid?" I'm all for being direct and was certain he would say he did just want to get laid. He disagreed and said he would actually like to take me out on a date in L.A. and that he was willing to drive to visit me.

We danced a bit more; I kissed him a couple of times, and gave him my number. We had to leave, after all we're in our 30's and it was after midnight. He called, without fail, the following day. I wonder…why, why, why do the one's you want to call not call and the one's who shouldn't call do call? Unbelievable. He actually left me a very sweet message saying he liked having met me and enjoyed talking to me and hoped that I'd had a safe drive home.

I called him; we talked for a while, and ultimately agreed that we'd go on a date the following week. He'd never been to my part of town and was interested in exploring it. So, we made our date. Well, I sat on this for about four days and realized I didn't see any point to this. The only reason it would have been helpful to me at that point was that he could have been a distraction from another man that I was interested in.

The irony was that, just as I was leaving to go to lunch with Shane (who was really at the peak of my interest at the time), my phone rang and it was my young dance partner from San Diego. He had just called to say hello and wish me a good weekend. I was literally running out the door and didn't have time to tell him how I felt so I just said I'd talk to him later. The following day I called him and we talked and I shared with him how I felt and he said he understood. He said to me, "I *thought* you'd back out." So, there you have it. I may have learned my lesson about long distance dating after all.

15

MEETING AND DATING FRIENDS OF FRIENDS

I think one of the most exciting and frustrating and nerve-racking situations are when friends set up friends. The outcome can be one of a number of possibilities, but one sure thing is a potential risk for the middle person. Personally, I haven't minded setting up my friends and don't seem to mind the risk.

The most recent and positive friends of friends experience for me occurred when I'd just stopped dating someone. I had just turned thirty. I was in the dumps, depressed, frustrated, pissed off, and not in a good way at all.

Lizbeth said to me one night, when I had forced myself to agree to go out with my other friend Holly, "I have a little something for you that will make you feel better. He's such a cutie. You just want to eat him all up and I can't have him since he works for me…I know you'll like him. His name is Andy. He's only 22 but, he is so adorable and this is what you need…he's my assistant." Now, I wasn't looking for a fling and I told her as much but I figured I'd think about it. Timing, after all, is everything. Lizbeth was going out that night with him and another co-worker in the same part of town as I was. We decided to talk later that night and potentially convene.

We all ended up getting together. And, boy was she right. She definitely knows my taste. He had a rugged quality, surfer-look, beautiful eyes, a great smile, good body, and a real manly look…as if he could whittle.

Andy seemed intrigued by me also. We had a couple of drinks and went out to eat. I did bring him home, and again a man makes a toothbrush reference. I did have an extra one. Maybe it is good to keep a stash after all, for friends, lovers, loved ones, *and* one night stands. We came home late, intoxicated, and talked at length. Turns out he had a pretty rough and hard upbringing and had been around the block. He had a sense of wisdom and intensity about him that made him all the more attractive and seem much older than his birth age.

Ultimately, we did end up making out and fooled around and had a great time together. The best part was that he helped pull me out of my funk—I called him an angel the following day when we were discussing our meeting, our lives, and the timing of our acquaintance. We added some handwriting analysis, just for fun. He was complimentary, reassuring, and a total stud. We talked about knowing what our purpose was in meeting one another. He had hit a lull, was isolating a lot, and was not in a good place. I gave him a boost by complimenting him (how could I not?). It was a great connection and very comfortable. He took me to breakfast and we had a nice time. We parted ways and I was left feeling as though a weight was lifted off of me and that an angel had dropped down on me from heaven.

We saw each other once again when a group of us went out (all women) and included him. He sure was a lucky man. We played games, drank wine, went out to dinner, and he stayed over again. I only saw him one other time when I paid a visit to Lizbeth at her work. It would have been nice to hang out with him a bit more since he was a safe and comfortable distraction and a nice person at that. After our rendezvous, it was as if he was recharged because, according to Lizbeth, he could not seem to get enough of women. Obviously our paths were meant to cross.

Another friend of a friend connection I had left me less content. A group of us went out dancing one night, and I gravitated to Gary, who could dance (a total turn on). He had Argentinean blood. He ended up coming home with me, made no requests for a toothbrush and we fooled around but didn't have sex. We really had a great time. He then called me a day or two later and asked me out on a date. We went to dinner and then to a pub and spent a number of hours together. It was a lot of fun. He was affectionate, intelligent, easy to talk to, and it was very comfortable. He dropped me off and we made out a little bit.

So, a few days passed and I didn't hear from him. I figured that's fine. I then decided to call to say hello and left a message. I didn't hear back again. Nothing. Nada. I thought that it was strange so I left another message, knowing he wouldn't be there and said I'd just wondered why and if he could leave me a message and let me know what was up. Never heard from him again. I learned a full year later that he'd felt he had to "run." This shocked me. The irony is that I don't think I could've been any more casual. I guess it just wasn't right. At least I got a nice dinner and date out of it.

I have a male friend, Jordan, who is single and interested in meeting people. He's someone I've known for almost 20 years and we wouldn't be compatible with one another in a relationship. A few years ago, because I love to set people up, I decided to set him up with a woman friend of mine, Gaile, from a different circle. They talked and decided that he would come over to her place and just hang out. It turns out it wasn't a match for either. Interestingly, she wasn't attracted to him, nor was he to her. What I did find interesting, however, was that she wore sweats, no makeup, and was ultra casual. Now, I am all for that but I also know that initially men are attracted to the physicality of women and that women need to do a little primping to accommodate this innate nature of men. I don't whether the circumstances would have been different if she had dressed up, but at least I tried.

Following this instance by about a year later, Jordan and Jess both attended a party I threw. They were attracted to one another, hit it off, and exchanged numbers. He called and asked her out and they had a great time together. He then called her again and they went out. He indicated he wished to see her again. Guess what? No call. Nothing. Never heard from him. I haven't a clue as to what the deal was. Our philosophy is that he just wasn't in a place to pursue a relationship. It also may have been the case that he was looking for something more physical and because she didn't put out, he lost interest.

Jordan, at a different time, ended up hanging out and fooling around a bit with Eve. I think, over the years, there had always been some interest and curiosity on both ends. They spoke again and he indicated he was going to Mexico for the weekend and asked her if she cared to join. How could she pass this up, she thought. So, he said he'd call and he totally flaked. Never called. Nothing. Boy, was she pissed. Fortunately, they've not seen each other since and I'd just assume not be around them when they do. It may be quite uncomfortable.

There was another man, Dale, who I met a few years back at a restaurant with a bunch of work colleagues. It was a table of about ten women and we ended up talking with two men. Dale was a real sweetheart, from out of town, was a physical trainer, and an ex-military guy. We hit it off and hung out a couple of times after that. There was never a real interest on my end and I sort of dropped the ball. Didn't talk again. Literally, a couple of years later, there I am, walking in my neighborhood and lo and behold, there he is, driving by. This was hysterical; we rekindled a friendship and were once again in contact, without any physical element.

So, New Years Eve came about and my three girlfriends, Jess, Sasha, and Annie, were to hang out with me. Dale came along and we all had a blast, hitting up a couple of parties. Jess and he sort of hooked up. They ended up spending the next day together and had a great time. Then they hung out once more and nothing ever really developed out of it. No big deal. This is just what happens sometimes. I haven't talked to him since and I'd say it's been about a year and a half. Just recently, he called Jess out of the blue and asked, "Who is this?" to which she replied, "Who's this?" He said, "It's Dale Smith." She then asked him, "What are you doing, cleaning out your black book?" "Yes," he said…"Just lose the number!" she said. He just hung up, not seeming to have a clue as to whom he'd called.

Kent, my friend from work, is single, my age, and a nice, intelligent and attractive man. I thought a while back of setting him up with Joy. They both expressed interest and they hung out a couple of times. They had a nice time, enjoying each other's company. Then, he just didn't call. Whenever I'd talk with him, he always had something positive to say about her. He did call her once and left a message. Nothing developed between them.

The funny thing about all of this is that he has hooked up with two of my friends casually. He met Jess at a party a couple of months after he'd met Joy. I'm thinking, and I told him as much, he owes me big time. Funny story though, that he's met two women, at various times, both extremely different from one another, through me. People have asked why I never pursued him. Simply, we work together and we're not attracted to one another in that way.

My last friends of friends story has made me laugh every time I've told it. The Navy Seal I mentioned, Cody, was to do a stint in Kodiak, Alaska of all places. Believe it or not, Meliss and Delia, lived in Kodiak at the same time. I facilitated a meeting with Cody and Delia. I also encouraged her to try out the goods. He was interested in meeting them and they him and his Team pals. They ultimately all hooked up and had a blast. She was forever grateful for having met him and they really enjoyed each other. I'm glad I was willing and able to share. Maybe some day he will be a gigolo.

16

THE BENEFITS OF FRIENDS IN TOW

Friends can really come in handy when hoping to meet someone or trying to pick up on someone. I have found that, time and time again, I have benefited from having my friends with me because I tend to have an easier time beginning and maintaining conversations when I am not alone. I am not about to randomly walk up to a man and strike up a conversation on my own, but if I have a woman with me I might be so inclined. Less pressure. Less on the spot. After all you have your wingman/woman.

I know from experience that it helps to have a friend around. For example, for a couple of years, I was a member at the same gym as Sasha and Jess. We would work out together, have fun, goof around to lighten things up a bit. And almost always, there were opportunities to engage in conversation with various men. The men would initiate or I would feel more inclined doing so then had neither of my friends been with me. Unfortunately I had to switch gyms and now I work out alone. I rarely talk to any of the men at my gym. Of course, I am going to the gym to work out, not to flirt. But, it sure would be nice if I happened to meet someone there.

Sasha and I went to sushi one night. We sat at the sushi bar. Two men sat down near us and we struck up a conversation. We discussed age and names, swapped drivers licenses…you know, typical initial talk. We told them that we hadn't determined our final destination for the night. One guy said that he was interested in joining us while his friend said he was beat and ready to retire. So, we left it that he might join us or we might join him, in his hot tub mind you, and that we'd talk in a bit after we went our separate ways. We parted. Sasha and I discussed that we both thought the guy was cute and all, but she said she was not really interested. I did talk to the guy later, but never ended up seeing him.

The plus though is that when with a friend, you can meet more than one person easily and compare notes about who could be compatible with whom.

Taking friends to places where you are likely to find men or women like you is a good idea. Joy and I once decided to place ourselves in an environment that we were both fond of: a surf spot. This way we could appreciate beautiful surfers. So, there we were when I saw a really attractive guy, but opted not to do anything. I kept staring (the benefit of dark sun glasses) and he eventually walked over to ask us for something. We then took the ball and began conversing with him. He was a real sweet guy. We both found ourselves attracted to him and it appeared he felt the same. It was exciting yet awkward. We ended up making plans for the three of us to hang out that night.

Joy and I sat there, looking at each other, and thought aloud, "what a random situation!" We were basically going on a three-person date! How the hell did that happen? We were both nervous, both excited, and we both wondered who was in to who and what we should do! We decided that we were lucky because we were together and could experience dating someone we didn't know as a pair! This totally took the edge off! We agreed that we would both be happy for the gal who connected with. This was so reminiscent of the time when we developed a multitude of hand signals for a comedy singles event two years prior! The things we women do never cease to amaze me!

Laughing at our unusual situation, we went to our respective homes to shower and change and then we finally met up for dinner. It was during dinner that I felt a shift in my interest, which was for the better because the two of them seemed to be connecting a bit more. They dated for a while. It all worked out for all of us. Had she and I not been there together, we never would have met him, and how nice for at least one of us to be able to go for it with him. Nothing like having a friend around. With a friend by your side, there is often less of a fear rejection or discomfort. It's similar to tripping in front of a bunch of strangers while walking alone (horrifying and embarrassing to most) versus the same scenario with a friend next to you (funny, entertaining, sometimes hysterical).

I experienced the benefit of having good friends in tow while at the beach once in San Diego. We saw this really cute guy by himself. He left and was gone for a long period of time, leaving his towel and stuff behind, clearly to return at some point. We wanted to talk to him but didn't know what to say. So, there we were, the three stooges...we took his towel and moved it closer to us...literally. This way we had easier access to him and were able to have a conversation upon his return. Of course, he was visiting from out of town (this seems to happen to all 3 of us frequently) and was a real gem. At least we found out and had a nice conversation at that. Again, none of us would have ended up talking to him had any of us been alone.

17

WORK DATING AND ATTRACTION: DON'T BRING SAND TO THE BEACH

People say that you often meet people at work. I have to say that, for me, this method for meeting people has backfired. After graduate school, I worked in a hospital setting. Over the three years I worked there, I dated five co-workers. One experience was with a guy named Mitch whom I was very attracted to, with whom I worked infrequently. Most people were attracted to him. We became friendly, hung out, and hit it off. He was a bit of a tripper but such a nice guy. We did end up sleeping together in the early stage of our friendship and it was great. What followed was confusion on my end as to what the outcome might be.

He wasn't anywhere near looking for a relationship and he and I just remained friends. We would flirt, talk about sexual issues, personal and not, and always got along really well. It was very frustrating a lot of the time. I found myself having difficulty focusing on my work at times, fantasizing about him, and calculating conversations more than I care to admit. I always wondered since we were compatible, sexually attracted to one another, and shared our analytical prone nature, than why, why, why, couldn't we be dating or in a relationship? This seems to be a question that comes up for a lot of women who are presented with the single life. As much as I always wanted a brother, I'd much rather have a lover and not be like a sister to someone. It was a great friendship while it lasted and there was always intense chemistry between us. We did speak of fooling around again at various times, but it never did occur. We talk about once a year, and he is still single, as far as I know.

At this same place, in which I had a tremendous amount of learning to do, I also had an experience with another man. He was very attractive, sweet, and cool.

He asked me out, and we went to a movie and dinner. I think what happened was that I didn't feel we had enough in common and we worked at the same facility. Though we didn't work together much, I knew it was bound to go nowhere and I sure as hell didn't want anything to do with sleeping with another person from work.

At this hospital, there were a variety of people because it was a large facility. There was one doctor in particular, Jake, who was not particularly attractive, but there was something sexy and mysterious about him. I can't quite remember how we came to talking. I knew he was significantly older and that he had a really nice car. I'm not one to go for the status of a person, nor am I one to like significantly older men, but somehow I got hooked. I was caught up in the flattery, and I was curious about this man who had seemed so unattainable. We went to lunch once. What followed, on our second date, was a visit to his home. I am pretty disgusted when I think about it, and saddened for that matter. Jake was extremely narcissistic and needed to show me all of the intricate details of his house. It actually was not a house but a mansion of sorts complete with a bed that lit up and an enormous walk-in closet made of mahogany. I could go on and on. Regardless, he was a man with a bad reputation and I learned this after only these two dates. From that point on, I had merely a cordial relationship with him.

Then of course there was the token married (but separated of course) man, Lane. He was sexy, sweet, high energy (like myself), about the same age, a bit juvenile, and had experienced a very different lifestyle than me. He pursued me and we ultimately did hang out. Throughout this time I knew he was separated and most likely getting a divorce. Fortunately, this tryst did not result in the typical scenario of the woman waiting for the man in hopes he'll divorce his wife, which never happens. It was actually more that I knew he wasn't for me and that I did not have any interest in sharing his type of lifestyle. He became a bit obsessive and neurotic. I concluded that part of his appeal for me was that I was almost the exact opposite of his wife. I was intriguing to him, the woman with friends, with no responsibility, I could be "free," go out and party, and have fun. He, on the other hand, had a child and was trapped, or so he felt.

Over time, Lane came to grips with the fact that he was going back to his wife and that he was going to make the best of it. But, strangely, he started flirting like crazy with all sorts of women but kept them at arms length. Fortunately, we were able to end up as friends. He was an awesome guy, but needed to make a decision about what he was doing with his life. Was he going to be in his relationship and be a family man or leave and have the single life? I also think it is important here to mention the fact that people can get trapped by having children early on and sometimes this works, but sometimes it doesn't.

At this same hospital, I also developed an interest in another man named Jed. He was actually 19 years older than I, divorced, with a nine-year-old, and he was my boss. Looking back, I think there was something appealing about his wisdom and experience. We had a conversation in which he disclosed his attraction and I did the same. We then spent a couple of afternoons together. He was an amazing man. I do believe that it may have worked had we been closer in age and had we not worked together. He told me that people at our work were suspicious though nothing had happened on the physical front, and that his boss, the CEO, had read him his riot act. It took me a while to make sense of it and move on. We ultimately were friendly and had a good working relationship. Actually, a couple of years later, after I'd left the work place, we ended up getting together for dinner, he and myself still single, and we had a wonderful time. For the first time, after having known each other for about four years, we did end up fooling around. No intercourse but definite physical activity.

In the interim, I worked at another facility, affiliated with the job. It was there that I met a man with whom I worked regularly. His name was Nelson. He was incredibly sexy. He was also with a child and a few years younger than me. Though a shy and tentative man, he and I became friendly and there was an intense chemistry between us. Neither of us acted on it but there was always a temptation. About a year after my departure, I too talked with him and the door was left open to see one another. I knew, however, that there was no reason other than being sexual with him, that I should see him again. I haven't talked to him since.

What I did learn from this particular place of employment is that people thrive on drama and search for any reason whatsoever to talk about people and feed off of suspicions. I provided an avenue for people to do this because of the men. People at various times had suspected something having gone on with all of them. I wish I could say that I learned that messing with fire at the workplace wasn't such a good idea. I will say, though, that it was a time in which I did feel incredibly flattered. Five incredibly different men were interested in me at some point during this time. And, I got involved briefly with a dangerously manipulative narcissist. I think the trick is to not get caught up in the flattery of co-workers and to be mindful of the potential for gossip.

Workplaces that allow for co-workers to wear swimsuits and be outside only heighten the temptation to break company policy about dating colleagues. I mentioned earlier the Navy Seal fetish. Well, the summer after I had my fling with

Cody, I worked at a camp for kids. At this camp there was a hottie named Connor who, was scheduled to begin training for the Seals when camp finished at the end of the summer. This guy was incredibly sexy, ripped, beautiful, so edible. Of course I was beside myself with attraction. Now, he wasn't all that bright, nor did I fit the mold that he was attracted to. However, initially, in the pre-camp training, a bunch of us went out and partied. He and I did end up hanging out and made out a bit. I wish I could say that I enjoyed a whole summer of physical pleasure with him. Nothing ever happened again. I lusted after him and couldn't help myself with this intense preoccupation. I'd talk to others about it, fantasize about it, and have wishful thinking and the like. But, nothing ever happened. C'est la vie. He was a good guy and I think did make the Seals.

A few years prior I'd worked at another camp. At this place I was a lifeguard and was friendly with a man from Australia, Reed, who was on a work visa for the summer. He was awesome and fun and we had a blast. Nothing happened between us and we still, about ten years later, have the enjoyment of communicating by email. I, to this day, wonder what would have happened if he were an American. We've talked about it but that is all. I haven't yet resorted to a move across the world. Maybe this will change if we are both single ten years from now. As they said in an episode of friends, it's always good to have a backup. I hope I'll never have to resort to the use of a backup.

Now, it was about five years after I'd worked at the camp and I was in the grocery store with my roommate. I see this fine man, so sexy, smooth skin. I smiled and continued walking. Damn. I thought he looked familiar. I am one of those individuals who is either blessed with or cursed with, depending on how you look at it, never ever forgetting a face. We crossed paths again and he approached me with a smile. He then said, "Hey, we worked at camp together a few years ago, what was your name again?" It was then that it clicked. He did remember me well and insisted that we get together soon. We exchanged numbers and I told him that we were going to have a party in the next week and that he should come. He did come, and with an agenda. He wanted to get down big time. It was at this time that there were a lot of other things going on with different men in my life and I was a bit confused. He was actually a potential catch but again, I felt that we weren't necessarily compatible and I also didn't want to have meaningless sex. We did make out that night, attempted a few times to hang out with one another and ultimately lost contact.

About two years ago, I started working at a school. I found, during the first month or so, as a part-time employee, that there were three men who I found particularly attractive. Damon was a surfer and the quiet type. I couldn't ascertain if he was egotistical or shy. Then there was a very tall one, Tyler, and another surfer, skateboarder type, almost 40, Lane.

One would think that after my failed love interests at the hospital and at camp that I wouldn't involve myself on a personal level with anyone at work. Well, somehow being around all the hot teachers at school made me forget my regrets and the difficulties at the hospital. I think it was in part because a couple of years had passed and it had been a while since I had had a relationship.

I found myself quite pleased that there were these cuties on the premises and ultimately developed a friendship with the skater, Lane. I got to know the "tall man", Tyler, because a few students I worked with were in his classes and because I passed him periodically on the P.E. field. Damon and I interacted only once or twice and he made no effort to get to know me.

By the end of the school year, I had a strong crush on Tyler. I had an attraction to him and found him to be interesting, entertaining, and curiously appealing. So, my gossipy friend told him there was someone interested in him in an effort to ascertain whether he was still with his girlfriend or not. He was. On my last day of work before the summer, Tyler and I had a conversation that touched on relationships and related issues. He told me that his relationship was challenged in some ways. I disclosed to him that I had been interested in him but that I never did anything with it because I knew he was in a relationship. Because this was my last day of work for a couple of months, I let him know that if anything were to change, that he should let me know. I heard from him a month later.

He called and it turns out that he and his girlfriend had "sort of" broken up. I thought, wow, is this cool or what! I had already reflected on our last conversation and had felt pretty excited about him. As is common of a rebound, I was almost the opposite of his ex. After talking for some time, we made plans. He was looking to buy a car near my apartment. So, we made a date; we went for dinner and ended up watching TV and ultimately fooling around. We had a passion filled summer together and continued to see each other secretly when school resumed.

The frustrating piece was that no one at work knew we were dating. He was actually not only dating me, but also another P.E. teacher at that school. I'd suspected this all along but he continued to deny it. He claimed to want to keep our relationship private so as not to contribute to the typical work environment rumor mill. The lesson for me, and maybe for a reader or two, is to PROMISE to never date anyone from work again. It took a few times, but I got the lesson.

18

SHHHHH!!!!!!

I think that, having covered dating co-workers, it is appropriate to address the issue of keeping a relationship secret. People thrive on drama and chaos at times, and gossip in workplaces and social groups is common. Admittedly, I love to learn of and hear what is going on with other people, but I can also see the spiritual and practical pitfalls of engaging in gossip.

The hospital where I worked was ridden with gossip. I could not tell anyone about the men I dated there. This extremely gossipy environment was difficult for me, but I was able to keep most things to myself. I was concerned for my personal and professional reputation.

At school, Tyler kept our relationship from all of our co-workers. I had become close to one of his female colleagues and I couldn't even tell her when he and I started dating. Ultimately, after time had passed, I was able to divulge the whole story to her. She wished I'd told her earlier but I stuck to my word and didn't tell her about it at his request.

I think the most difficult experience for me was the situation with Tyler at the school and his request that we never tell anyone about our relationship. Over the first year that I knew him, three people mentioned that they thought we would be a great couple. When he and I did start going out, I was dying to tell them, as I'd been so excited. They would have been ecstatic. During the time that Tyler and I were going out, co-workers often asked him and me separately whether we were dating anyone.

Friends of mine outside of work thought it suspicious that he chose to be so private about us, but I felt I should respect his privacy. I know, looking back, that there was some gain for him in keeping his life private and "unknown." He loved to be mysterious, and he loved having people be intrigued by him.

The most difficult stage of our covert relationship was when we stopped going out and I struggled with the loss. I had spent every weekend with him having sex and enjoying each others company, and then it abruptly stopped. I continued to interact with him because we did work in the same place. When I learned three months after our breakup that he was dating the other woman I had always been suspicious of, I was shocked and more upset that he had insisted on keeping "us" a secret. I decided that one thing I did learn is that if I have to keep a relationship at work private, there can be ramifications and discomfort during the relationship and after, if it ends.

Jen also dated a man she met in a social club. They really had a wonderful time pursuing one another and enjoyed each other's company. No other people in the club were aware of their dating. The couple felt exposing their relationship might be uncomfortable for them and others. They dated in secret for a few months. Ultimately, their relationship fizzled and they became acquaintances. She avoided him at a variety of events where she knew he might be and was uncomfortable hearing positive and gossipy things about him from others in the group.

On the brighter side, I am aware of a few instances where secret relationships succeeded. I have a friend, Amber, who is now married and has two children with a man she met at work. They were quiet about their relationship for a couple of years partly because she had previously dated someone else there. She and her husband disclosed their relationship when they moved in together. It does fascinate me that they were able to sustain secrecy for so long. This takes a great deal of will power. They are happy together and have no regrets for having gone about their lives in the fashion they did. They still work together.

Another girlfriend of mine, Sherry, also met her fiancé at work. Again, no co-workers knew, they kept it "hush hush" and were extremely slick about the whole thing. Fortunately it wasn't longer than a year after they'd begun dating that she left and began working elsewhere. He no longer works there either. They are now extremely happy. They'll be getting married within the next year or so.

Lastly, Eve began dating a man at church whom she has known and been friends with for seven years. At a certain point, they took into account life changes, time, their maturity, and discussed that they were interested in one another and they began to date. The have been inseparable ever since. The catchy part is that though they see each other a minimum of two times weekly for church related events, no one at church knows they are dating. This secrecy at church seems a bit more difficult to understand, but, according to Eve, were their relationship to be public, the congregation would have a field day gossiping about it. I believe it would be cathartic for them both if they shared their love for one another with the people that are close to them.

My belief is that people figure out what is best for them and they do what they feel comfortable. It is fascinating to think that there may be many people we interact with daily who are dating that we don't know about.

19

INTERNET DATING EXPERIENCES

In pursuit of the ideal man, with encouragement from friends, I looked for love in cyberspace for a couple of years. I would have to say that, overall, the men I met were nice and nothing too tragic or really odd happened. What did happen was I met a lot of people and learned even more about myself than I already knew. When one goes through unfamiliar or intimidating experiences, one often finds an opportunity for growth. I would have to say that the insight I gained into myself was the most valuable part of my entire Internet dating experience. My cyber dating experience produced a variety of funny little stories that I find worth sharing here.

I need to preface this by saying that I learned a few important things that I'd like to offer to anyone, man or woman, who intends to pursue a relationship via the Internet. Seeking and corresponding is a very time consuming adventure and one has to be up for the time and energy investment. Women especially need to be clear about their criteria and use a great deal of discretion. Women tend to get numerous responses, and they have to go through a weeding out process. Using a system, like a preliminary set of criteria, can limit the sense of being overwhelmed and abandoning the whole idea.

Patience is also of utmost importance because this is a very intensive process and can take some time. If you are prone to nervousness or anxiety, I would suggest figuring out how to ease these feelings. As a woman who is outgoing, gregarious, social, and talkative I had a tremendous amount of anxiety and worry before meeting my dates. Even though I had talked with the person on the phone prior (this is a definite necessity) I often got very nervous before hand. Once I met them I was fine; it was just the anticipation. Be aware of false advertising and watch out for ads that embellish. Men often complain that women would describe themselves as curvy only to find our they are actually round, while women complain of men adding at least two inches to their height.

On the positive side, you have the opportunity to weed through people without having to interact in a phony fashion as you sometimes find yourself doing at a bar or singles event. You can quickly learn a great deal about a person and their interests and whether or not he/she is a match for you. You also get the opportunity to meet a number of people, some who may turn out to be friends. And, it is imperative here that I mention I hear at least once a year of a successful relationship that began on the Internet. I am happy to say one of my dearest friends has met the love of her life on the Internet.

In the beginning of my experience exploring Internet dating, I got e-mails from numerous men inquiring about my ads. I wasn't interested in many of them. I tried to be polite and sensitive in my correspondence when I was clear that I wasn't interested. However, the e-mails I got back were often surly. When I politely indicated that I was not interested in one man, his response was that I was a "bitch and a whore and a terrible person and a representation of women being horrible people." He was so hostile that his response could be classified as verbal harassment. Calling him the "Angry Internet Man" to this day, it is my belief that women should be aware of this potential scenario when utilizing the Internet as a means with which to meet others. My suggestion to women who encounter this situation is to let the Internet site know about the harassing e-mails and to forward it to them.

Instant messaging seems to be something that can both work for and against someone. What happened to me was that I got instant messages regularly from men because they were interested and curious. Unfortunately, I didn't have the time or interest to look up every man's profile and/or respond. I then learned that blocking everyone other than specific people whose messages I wanted to receive was the way to handle the onslaught of messages. I would keep this in mind because, once there is any communication via e-mail, you can then be put on any user's buddy list.

My most memorable Internet dating experience was at an Italian restaurant with a man named Dayton. The second date was filled with many mini horrors. We met at his house and went to dinner. When I arrived, right on time, I knocked and there was no answer. I waited for about thirty seconds and rang the doorbell. After at least another couple of minutes had passed, a very bed-headed Aaron opened the door, apologizing in an aloof fashion for having fallen asleep. He welcomed me by telling me to take a tour of my "soon to be home" while he proceeded to get dressed. I walked around, pet the fat furry Persian cat he had talked about on our first date, and took notice of his well kept home. He appeared and we got into the car. He was quiet, staring ahead at the road. I attempted to engage him in conversation by asking a question. He answered, curtly…I asked him if he was okay and he let me know, sharply, that he was "just tired and hungry and I just haven't awakened yet." I thought, well, this is a great way to start the evening.

It just didn't seem right that, on the second date, he was acting in this way. I thought, well, I just have to get through the night. We arrived at the restaurant and he was still quiet. He stared at me often, not saying a word, and never initiated any form of conversation. It was quite unpleasant. When we received the menus he exclaimed, "everything is great!" I asked him if he wanted to recommend anything in particular. He said I would do fine with whatever I chose. I took his answer literally and ordered my usual, spaghetti with marinara. I figured I'd ask to have some chicken added. When he asked what I had chosen and I told him, he looked at me in shock and said, "How could you order something like that when there are so many things to choose from on the menu." I wanted to sock him right there and say, "then why the hell did you tell me that anything would be great, asshole." But, I didn't. I figured I'd just go ahead and enjoy the meal. It never got better. We ate and the food was pretty darn good (at least I was exposed to new eatery) and we left for his house after skipping dessert.

When we arrived at his house, he clearly wanted to mess around. It was at that point that I'd realized this was bound to go nowhere quickly, at least not in the direction I'd wish for. So, after a lot of pushing on his part, I let him know I needed to leave, that I was tired. I figured he would empathize because he would be able to relate, after earlier having mentioned his tiredness. A couple of days later, I sent him an email letting him know that I was appreciative of dinner, but that it wasn't clicking for me and I wished him well in his future dates.

Seeing as I felt there was nothing to discuss, I figured he'd blow it off. Unfortunately, I was wrong. He called me at home late that night. I didn't answer and waited to see who was going to leave me a message. No message. Just a hang up. Throughout the night and into the early morning my phone must have rung about six times. It was insane. I then got a little worried. Finally, knowing this was bound to continue unless I put a stop to it, I called him. He was angry, frustrated, persistent, and couldn't take no for an answer. We were on the phone for about 45 minutes. He was trying to convince me that I'd not allowed enough time to see if we'd be a match. He began trying to sell himself to me, saying things like, "I like psychology and I just bought a treadmill." He was trying every angle and was telling me I was wrong. I just kept telling myself, "He is not well, he is dangerous, and thank God I hadn't given him my address." Finally, I got off the phone by telling him that I'd be willing to think more about it. That was all I was willing to do. So, I gave it a few days and then called, knowing there was a slim chance he'd answer (which he thankfully did not) and said I'd thought about it but that I felt the same way as a couple of days ago. Maybe one could call this an interesting experience or a lesson in not knowing what you sign up for when you meet someone through the Internet. There have only been a couple of men who I've felt comfortable enough to let know where I live. But, clearly, one needs to be very careful.

On the more positive side, I have had a number of dates with men who were nice, sweet, healthy, intelligent gentlemen. Unfortunately, I can't say that any of them were appealing physically. Here's my story about these men:

Vince: he was fun and entertaining and had high energy. He was bald and must've been not one inch taller than me. I don't mind a short man, nor do I mind a bald man necessarily. However, since neither are *preferences* for me, when there is a combination of the two, the chemistry isn't running through me. He asked me out again and I let him know I didn't feel the spark. He was disappointed but appreciated my candidness. We then agreed that if either of us had someone to set the other one up with that we should keep each other in mind.

Ron: I met a man who had been married and had a child who was about 7. He was well read, kind, worldly, and intense, all great and appealing qualities. He drove a cool car. He was a gentleman and must have been almost 2 feet taller than Vince. But, he was a bit nerdy. Additionally, though I had no judgment about it, he did stutter. This was a major distraction for me and made it hard to focus. He came from far away and spent the night. If I'd been willing, we could have had sex in a second. We cuddled and it felt nice, but he also seemed like such an over the top romantic that it felt almost clingy. I let him know, via email, that he was a special person but that it wasn't a match. It felt like we came from such different worlds. Believe it or not, I set him up with Joy because I felt they had more commonalities. He was grateful, as was she. They went out and had a nice time, but it wasn't a match for either of them. Hey, at least we all tried.

Steve: he was a real sweetheart, though not very bright. I didn't feel at all intellectually stimulated by him. If I remember correctly, he hadn't gone to college. He was also Middle Eastern, making for a different cultural background. We had a nice dinner but I felt bored out of my mind. I let him know that it didn't feel like a match and he was disappointed but accepting of it.

Paul: a real nice guy, very bright, a doctor, surfer, funny, but sort of flat on the phone. I had built this guy up to be something quite different than what he was.

I felt pretty bored by him also. Not much of a connection, just feeling like being worlds apart. He also had some sort of distracting growth on his face and, admittedly, it was hard not to stare. I am not a shallow person, but I must say that I felt shallow that day. We drank beer and played pool and then took a walk. He wanted to continue to hang out but I told him I had to be somewhere. I never heard from him again. I think he got the picture.

Kurt: This guy was high energy, funny, witty, lived a mere 2 blocks away, and seemed entertaining enough. We met and he had that more alternative, funky look. Not a bad look, just not one I'm usually drawn to. So, there we were, eating breakfast, me already knowing and feeling he wasn't for me. It was a tad bit awkward but I managed to get through the meal. I definitely felt as though he was feeling as I was and I never heard from him again. I've always wondered if and when I might run into him. I've yet to even though it's been about 3 years.

George: He was another man who claimed to be a surfer. He was worldly, smart, successful, and persistent. Interestingly, he sounded sexy despite his flatness on the phone. The reality was that, again, I was caught up in my surfer-fetish. I was honestly floored when I saw him. So shocked. He was nothing like I'd expected nor did he look much like his picture. I also felt like there wasn't much we were connecting on. He was sort of bizarre. So, he wanted to continue to hang out but I told him I had to leave. I then sent him the token thanks but no thanks e-mail.

I met another man who seemed great in many ways on the phone. He had high energy, was successful, funny, entertaining, self-actualized, and very pro-relationship. When we met, he was wearing a Lakers jersey. I guess this sort of bothered me and seemed a bit cheesy. But, I sat there and tried to not focus on that. I think if I'd felt at all attracted to him, this wouldn't have been an issue. But, again, I wasn't attracted to him. I called him and let him know I wasn't interested. The funny side note was that he was some producer of pornographic flicks. I found this to be quite entertaining. This had made for some interesting conversations of course. I had also met another guy who was also a surfer. He wanted to take me to Indian food. He was nice and sweet and pleasant enough on the phone. Again, I met him and his mouth must have been a quarter of mine in size (I don't have a large mouth). He was also unbelievably flat; he had no affect. (What is it with these flat surfers?) I was bored to tears. He also had allergies (Indian spicy food didn't seem to help) and was sniffling and blowing his nose throughout the meal. I just didn't feel any attraction to him. I sent him an e-mail.

I met a guy who also seemed pleasant and interesting on the phone though he made these funny noises. I found this to be entertaining initially, especially because I tend to make funny noises also. Interestingly, again, he lived even closer than Kurt. This guy actually lived on my street. Unbelievable. We decided to meet and walk down the street for a drink. I saw him and wanted to run the other way. He had, in his ad, placed 5 pictures. He looked very different in all of them; this leaves a lot for interpretation. He looked good in one and fair in the others. Well, he was basically a total nerd. Not offensive, just not what I am attracted to. So, there I was, stuck. So, I tried to stay positive and open to the experience. We arrived at the restaurant and we just wanted a drink, maybe some nosh, but no meal per say. So, we get there and he actually asks if there is a table fee to sit at a regular table. I guess I thought this was weird. After all, many might find this a tad bit offensive. Maybe it's an east coast thing I don't know about. Then we talk about food and eating habits. He was a rail. We discuss other issues and clearly were not seeing eye to eye. He walked me home and asked me out again. I said yes and emailed him the following day apologizing for not being more direct (it's hard when you're on the spot) but letting him know it wasn't a match for me.

My very first Internet date was with a doctor, a bit narcissistic, and somewhat boring in my mind. We had coffee and talked a bit. At the end of the dated he said, "thank you for meeting me but I just don't feel like we're a match." I was pleased I didn't have to say this and that he'd beat me to it; it sure did take a load off. It was a little awkward though. Fortunately, we both agreed that we weren't a match.

I think the most interesting and entertaining blind date was with a 38 year-old man from Australia. He was sarcastic, intelligent, witty, sharp, entertaining, and all around fun to talk to. We attempted to get together, but because of our conflicting schedules and us living a bit of a drive from one another, it took a while to finally connect. He actually didn't want to drive in the rain because he had a Z3 and didn't feel safe in a downpour. What was bothersome, however, independently of the car situation, was that he was promoting I drive to see him. I guess I didn't feel comfortable with that. Though I wouldn't describe myself as very traditional, I still felt like the man should at least pursue and put a little effort into the conquest, an example being willing to drive. So, we never hooked up.

A bit of time passed and he e-mailed me again, asking for a second chance. We then decide to meet, him coming to my side of town. We met at a restaurant and had Patron tequila shots and some great food. I must say I'd never had this particular drink before but I loved it. We kissed a little bit and ate and drank and drank. He was too persistent though, and I could feel that he was the possessive, obsessive, bull-headed type of guy and I can't put myself in that position. I learned this at an early age. Fortunately, I'd set the night up in such a way that I had plans with some friends because another friend was in town. So, I had to leave. I said goodbye and heard from him the following day. I called him soon thereafter and told him it just wasn't a match for me. Of course, I was concerned that he might respond in the way the psycho-guy had, but much to my surprise, he was kind about it despite his disappointment.

The odd and almost hysterical addendum to this story is something that just happened recently. I'd decided, after about a two-year break, to revisit the Internet dating thing, using a different site. I received an email from a 40 year-old Australian, I opened the picture, and THERE HE WAS! It was the same man! He seemed to have not a clue about me, or so it seemed, because his writing to me never addressed the fact that we'd met before. It's classic. I think that really takes the cake. I guess there's a lot of cycling, or recycling for that matter, in the cyberspace world if one gives it enough time. Needless to say, I didn't respond. He was a real red-light guy.

A girlfriend's friend had dated a guy a few times that she met on-line. Apparently things went well and then he disclosed to her that he didn't want a commitment. The funny part was that this same guy had emailed me to go on a date. What are the chances of that occurring? And, had I not shared the specifics of the guy and her girlfriend hadn't, we'd never have known. The funny part was that he'd donated his hair when he cut it to an organization for children with cancer. This was kind and generous and curious to me. My therapist asked me about the man and why I liked him thus far. I replied, "He donated his hair…" As I said this, she and I both chuckled and agreed that this sounded so bizarre as an appealing trait for someone one meets on-line. Though he and I never did rendezvous in person, it's even clearer that Los Angeles isn't such a big city after all.

20

BLIND DATES

Blind dates can have a vast array of outcomes, whether setups or Internet sought. Continuously, I hear about funny recounts, especially from women, so I thought I'd mention a couple of them here.

A few years back I'd been investigating switching my car insurance and had a phone conversation with a salesman who intrigued me. He was funny, from the area I grew up in and we had some similar interests and commonalities. Ignoring my suspicion that his phone flirting may have been part of his pitch, I contacted him the following day after I'd decided not to take the insurance. When I called him back and asked if he knew why I was calling, he said, "You're calling to ask me out." Though his answer may sound a bit presumptuous, I think it reflected more of a knowingness he had. Of course, I told him this was true and we made a date to go out to dinner. Mind you this was a blind date in the sense that I had never seen him. Somehow, I trusted the flow of our interaction.

He picked me up and I was pleasantly surprised. He was cute, sweet, funny, and well dressed. I really felt comfortable and at ease with him. We went to the *Cheescake Factory* and were seated outside for drinks while we waited for a table. We ordered drinks and they didn't come. I decided to get up and ask what the hold up was. Little did I know that the dark room I walked into was separated from the outside by a barely visible thin screen. A group of ten people were eating dinner on the other side of the screen. I literally walked right into the screen and knocked it on top of the entire table. I ended up rolled up in the screen, tangled, like I was part of a burrito. This had to have been the most humiliating experience I've ever had. I wanted to run away, but instead, with a bit of struggle detangling myself, I rose and ran back to the table. There my date sat, head down, laughing, embarrassed as hell, telling me "just don't talk to me right now." How about that for a first date story? As it turned out, the wait staff wasn't surprised; they indicated they were waiting for this to happen at some point to someone due to the dark lighting. This gave me a bit of a sense of relief. I inherited the nickname "screen." This nickname dually applied to me because I often screen my calls. This made the nickname that much more appropriate. Though things didn't work out between us in the long run, we are still able to laugh about it.

An odd blind date story involves my girlfriend Jess. She went on a blind date with a man and knew from the get go that this was not going to be a match. After all, she found him a tad boring and she wasn't attracted to him. Something about him was sort of feminine-like and she was a bit turned off by this. There just wasn't a real connection. So, she's thinking during the dinner (this may have been a mistake after all) that she should just get the hell out of there. He asks if she'd be interested in ordering dessert. She opts not to, not only because she wishes to leave, but also because she's full and not a real dessert person anyway. Well, the waitress brings out the dessert tray, the guy asks again, insisting they get something. So, Jess says, sick of his pushing, "Okay, anything but the banana cream pie." What did he do? He orders the banana cream pie, says, "Try it. You'll love it, trust me." So, interestingly, she sits there, dumbfounded and thinks to herself, well, "I guess he is not gay, he's just deaf." I think this really speaks to the concept of listening and how important it is.

Another girlfriend, Darla, recently had a funny blind date situation. She'd been conversing with two different men and had plans one night with one and a few nights later with the other. Date #1 took her out and they drank and drank and drank. She liked him, felt chemistry, but there were times when it was sort of dull during their conversation. So, she's vacillating, but has a nice little buzz and is trying to enjoy herself. She goes to the bathroom and returns, having looked at the menu and planning to order a little something. The guy then says, "I have to be honest…" She, of course, immediately thinks he's going to say that they should end the date…there's a pause and he then says, "There's nothing on the menu I'm really interested in."

There she was, cracking up to herself and thinking, well, let's just continue enjoying the night. They proceed to get liquored and eat a little bit. She realizes she's been paged, doesn't know who it could be, and thinks she must call this person back. Well, lo and behold, it was date #2, nearby and telling her he was in the neighborhood, having a beverage, and wanting to hook up. She, of course, has to play it off, be ultra casual, and pretend it isn't a guy with whom she has a date planned. And, she has to be coy with date #2 about what she's doing that very moment. She managed to get herself out of the situation and has since dated only one of them briefly. This provided a real solid source of entertainment for us as one might imagine.

Through work, I have been also set up a number of times. The problem is that none of these people knew me very well at the time and they wouldn't know not to set me up with these particular men. Interestingly, however, with two of the dates, both in a group situation to minimize the pressure and anxiety, I would've been open to going out again with them. I wasn't sure about them but I wasn't thinking they were definitely "no's." However, the two men's true colors showed to their respective matchmakers even more after the dates. Both seemed to have issues with commitment and a variety of other things. Maybe they didn't expect to meet someone they actually liked. Regardless, they both expressed interest in me after the dates, asked for my phone number, and nothing happened. Ultimately, this turned out to be for the better.

The same thing occurred with another set of friends, a couple I've known for some time. I actually trust them a great deal and we three and another friend went out to dinner. The bonus was that he's a fireman (you know how we feel about firemen). He said he'd like to go out again (I was unsure) yet he never made any contact. It leaves one to wonder if men are just often over ridden with this misconception that women will break if they're told the guy isn't interested. Or, maybe they truly are interested but it's not a priority at that moment in time. Regardless, what it comes down to is a very frustrating situation that women continue to be subjected to. This is not to say that there are not direct men. It just appears to be an enigma to come in contact with them. I practice what I preach. I will quickly let the man know, in some fashion, that I'm not interested because the reality is it really sucks to be misled.

I think the story that takes the cake (you'll see the irony here shortly) is one in which I'd been set up on a blind date with a co-worker's friend. Nice enough guy. I see him, however, and know it's just not a match but I decide to be open to the experience regardless (this seems to have become my motto). We ended up seated next to a threesome of a couple and a single man at the *Cheesecake Factory*. We have periodic interaction throughout the meal (they'd probably proceeded us by about thirty minutes). My back is to them, but occasionally I turn around. My date, however, is clearly not interested in talking to these strangers, nor does he seem to be happy with my doing so. Admittedly, they were much more entertaining than he and I was pretty bored.

Ultimately, he got up to go to the bathroom and left me there with the table of three and the single man made some comment about the guy being a bore and expressed frustration with him not being a bit more enthusiastic. Some more time passes, I'm bored silly and I decide to go to the bathroom. As I'm returning, walking back to my table, the single guy hands me a piece of paper with his phone number on it and says, "You should call me, I know you'd have a far better time with me if we went out." I was shocked, flattered, and pleased, and told him I'd call.

The date ended, I went home, and a couple of days later I called the guy. We spoke for a while and he told me he could tell I wasn't interested in my date and that he had seemed like a bore. It turns out the man had recently divorced, was living on a boat, did not live nearby, and he was at least twelve years older than me. We talked about meeting up but this never happened. I just was left with an amusing and flattering story from the *Cheesecake Factory*. This place seems to be quite the storybook for me with respect to dating.

Most recently, I went out with my friend Dan and his roommate, DJ. He wanted to set us up. To minimize the discomfort, I brought Darla along and we went out as a foursome. I suggest dating in groups; it really does take the edge off. We four hang out and have some drinks and we're all getting along fairly well…DJ looks a tad familiar but I don't mention this. After about an hour or so, we're all talking about sushi and this particular place we all like to go. It then hit me. I had been there the night before with Lizbeth and saw a guy walk in who struck me enough to give him a second glance. It was DJ!!!!! How odd is that? I bring it up to him and he skirts the issue, downplaying the coincidence that we three thought was pretty cool. As I'd suspected, Dan shared with me the following day, DJ was with a woman and felt awkward about discussing it. It wasn't a love connection anyway, so it wasn't too much of a disappointment.

21

FIRST DATES

Jen was retelling a very funny story of when she had been awaiting her date's arrival to take her out. She felt excited, primped, extremely anxious and as ready to go as she could be. She'd also just had her hair straightened and it was looking pretty darn cute. There she was, doing her makeup and BAM, a chunk of mascara in her hair. She panicked of course, didn't know what to do, attempted to remove it, with little time to spare. She then felt she had not choice but to cut the strand off. She literally chopped the portion of mascara-infested hair off to REMOVE the problem. She must have covered up the damage sufficiently because he didn't seem to notice.

The funny part is that she did have an okay time with this person and he asked her out again. She actually had decided that she really was not interested and did not want to pursue anything but she felt like she could at least go out and have an okay time. She wore no makeup, overalls, and her glasses. You would think that a guy might pick up the hint that the woman is not interested if she opts to wear this sort of get-up. We chuckle about this even today because it could be used as such a feeler for a man. Ironically, the guy was still interested. And, here we women moan about how we have to often be pleasing to the man's eye, especially in the early courting stages and yet here is a man who clearly doesn't care.

Jen also recently moved out of state and is making attempts to put herself out there and be bold. She met a man she knew was younger and they made plans to go to a football game. He was a coach and wanted to take her to a local high school game. So, she's sitting there, becoming more and more clear that she may actually be at least ten years his senior and, it turns out he's Mormon. Different religions can be quite a challenge to work out and this is one of those challenges she's not all that interested in working through. She, herself, subscribes to a more Buddhist philosophy and lifestyle, that being very unlike that of a Mormon's lifestyle. She's thinking, well, what do you know, here I am trying to be open and I sit with a Mormon boy at a high school football game. I mean how open are we women supposed to be? Needless to say, they haven't seen each other since.

I think the most humorous story of all is one of a different friend of mine, Kari. She had been set up with this guy and they'd talked on the phone about their plans. This guy called the chamber of commerce to inquire about what they could do and what activities could be planned. He completely planned the entire day from the places to the drive, to the times, to the site seeing specifics. He even had a list to show for it. Total over preparation. It seems there should be a balance between putting some thought into plans for a date and no thought at all.

Then there was of course the token weird person who I met one night while out with some friends. He was actually a friend of a friend. He was interesting and a bit odd. This didn't concern me so we made plans to go out on a date. We actually went to dinner at an interesting place and chatted. He was weird but talkative and wore an extremely extroverted bright shirt and had a funky way of dressing and carrying himself. I felt he was clingy and neurotic and was over the top complimentary. I know that even if I were very interested in this guy I'd still have had my concerns. But, regardless, he just didn't float my boat. I ended the date as soon as I could and finally we each went home. He called the following day and I returned the call. I told him that I was flattered by his interest and that he was a nice guy but that I knew myself well enough to know that it wasn't a match with him. I apologized and said it was nice to have met him and that I wished him luck. What did he do? He thanked me for being so honest, complimented me on that and said I'd handled "rejecting him" very well. What was great is that I'd also told him the truth.

I think this brings to the point the idea of rejecting someone and how it is negotiated. Unfortunately, I don't believe dating should be so difficult but it can be. Rejection shouldn't have to be difficult either but it can be. I do continue to advocate for directness and honesty in telling people when one isn't interested. After all, I would hope that what comes around goes around

The last story I can think of was when I did meet a man at a bar (yes, this has happened a few times). He was just leaving, smiled, said something to me, asked for my number and I felt good about him so I gave it to him. He called the next day and we talked a bit and we decided to go out. He took me to the *Cheesecake Factory* (now I'm thinking, this is really quite the date place!) and we had a pleasant time. He was very short (I think he was actually my height) and he was a cop. Now, I really don't know how realistic it is for me to be involved with a cop because I see our worlds as being far apart. Not to say I'm involved in illicit things or behavior that would be looked down upon, more to say how the value system of police officers differs from that of a social worker, for example.

Anyway, I wasn't sure about him and we drank and fooled around and I felt very male about the whole thing. I was horny, not interested, and figured we'd have a one night fool around thing and that would be that. Well, quite the contrary occurred. He turned out to be very interested, was more attached, sensitive, and emotional. Unfortunately, as guilty as I felt, it just didn't feel right with him for me. There was something a bit odd about him. I really have had my share of odd men. So, I let him know. This was much more challenging for me in that he persisted and said I'd not given him a chance. He proposed we be friends. I declined because I didn't have interest in yet another friend. I was trying to be realistic in that I was busy with my social life and was hoping to meet a single available man appropriate for me with whom I connected. What also felt like a red flag to me was that he spoke to me as if we were really close and had known each other for years.

22

FAMILY HOOKUPS

I think the real interesting piece comes with the family matches. It gets to the point when one has to evaluate their situation and say to themselves, "I've had 100 set ups and at what point should I decide the type of man I want to go out with." Dating can be taxing, frustrating, and exhausting to say the least. My mother had a friend who managed an apartment building. She was nice, talkative, and fairly together. She told my mother of a tenant whom she thought was a real catch and whom she wanted to set me up with. Ultimately, after some back and forth, we were set up.

This man was nice, from back east, intelligent, a real gentleman, and interesting. However, there was no chemistry on my part and I didn't feel particularly comfortable. Not really that exciting. So, it didn't work out. But, heck, thanks to my mother for making that attempt seeing as she's yet to meet someone with whom she sees her daughter spending a date with.

Jess's mother is often looking and found some ads in the Jewish Journal. One man in particular stuck out for her for some reason and she actually called him. She basically did a preliminary interview with this guy on the phone, felt good about him and then told Jess about it. The long and the short of it was that her mother opted to play matchmaker and this resulted in a meeting half way (they lived two hours apart). It was not a match. But, again, thanks to the mothers for trying.

Then there are the grandparents. My grandmother has a friend who is a very hip and pleasant lady. She and I get to talking and it turns out her grandson is my age also. No, he was not single, but his best friend was. The woman spoke highly of him and we ultimately decided there would be a number exchange. He and I talked a few times on the phone, he was nice and we ultimately decided to meet. NOPE I thought to myself. This happens so often and I wonder if I am too closed but I tell myself I can't be because I've been attracted to men who aren't major head-turners. It's just an unexplainable chemistry thing. We tried to connect again but I ended up not trying hard enough and it sort of fizzled.

Lastly, I'm thinking of a recent situation in which my grandmother tried to facilitate something. She and my grandfather had been going to physical therapy for some time. They are in their 80's and are doing their best. Little did I know that their best was that of keeping a look out for their granddaughter. It turns out that I came up in conversation at their last physical therapy meeting because he is also single. He asked for a picture and I gave her one to bring to him the following day.

I wrote on the picture my address for him to return it if he wasn't interested. I told them to ask him to send me one. He neither sent me one nor sent mine back. This felt creepy. It had been a month or so and no picture, no mention, nothing. I ultimately had to involve my grandmother again so that I could get my picture back. It just felt funny to have my picture floating around in some guy's hands, someone I didn't even know. She got it back. He said nothing. Strange. But, it's nice to have grandparents trying. I feel lucky.

I also recently went to visit my aunt on a movie set and there was a man there who inquired about me after we had met and chatted a bit. He got my number and never called, much to my aunt's surprise, considering he seemed interested in me. I saw him again on the set and he asked her about me again. She told me I should call him. I did, we spoke a lot, had a good conversation and decided to hang out a week or so later. He never called. We never talked again. Really bizarre. But, it was nice that there was a venue through a relative to meet a nice guy.

23

BARS

Bars are notorious for funny situations, weird mishaps, and kooky, scandalous scenarios in the single world. I feel that I could probably write a book alone on the experiences my friends and I have had in bars.

One curious bar scenario involves meeting someone at a bar, and having quite different impressions of the person later after seeing them on the "outside" or hanging out with them. I remember a time when I was dancing with some friends at a bar and this man approached me. We ended up flirting, dancing, and hanging out most of the night. Later when it was time for us to leave we went outside and I saw him in the streetlight. My god! He looked seriously different outside in the light versus inside in the dark. I whispered to my friend that I had to get out of there and that is exactly what I did. I ran down the block and hid behind a dumpster. I was virtually peeing in my pants, laughing hysterically. Ultimately my friends caught on and I made a quick get away. I mean, I'm all for being direct but what do you do. You can't say, "I'm sorry, even though I've been hanging with you for the past two hours, I have now seen you in the light and I have changed my mind."

Once I was with a girlfriend of mine, Andrea, at a bar and we met these two men. They were both attractive and pleasant. We had a conversation that led me to identify one of the men as a "good egg." In my drunken state, I somehow managed to tell him a number of times that I thought he was a "good egg." We left the bar and went to a different bar and ended up at his house. We all hung out there and messed around a bit and then went home. I did see the "good egg" again, but never developed anything serous with him. Maybe the "good egg" comments turned him off or made me seem like his grandmother.

Bars that have pool tables offer ample opportunities for connections with the opposite sex and sexual antics. There is a clear high level of sexuality that equates with playing pool or billiards. Here you have a stick and balls flying all over the place; there are holes, people aim. Then you rub chalk on the stick. Here we have represented the penis, breasts, testicles, a vagina, and a clitoris. I knew there was a reason all my horny friends and I always loved this game.

Neighborhood dive bars are great bastions for dating. Kent has a roommate who recently opened a divvy sports bar called The Bitter Redhead. Conveniently it is right near my home. My friends and I have frequented "The Bitter" ever since it opened. The bar has a great dive bar quality and resembles a cool pub. The owners have told us about what they call the "bartender phenomenon." This is a universal phenomenon. Essentially, women hit on bartenders all the time. Women at this bar frequently write their names and numbers on napkins and give them to both men. I don't think I would ever feel comfortable dating a bartender because I would be quite concerned about the many women hitting on them.

Bar food as well as the drinks can create an allure too, though not as strong as the bartender. Jess and I once went to a mixer at a bar. There was a man at the end of the bar and who had ordered a pizza. Now, this pizza was HUGE, the man was alone, and he was quite slender. He sat there, nursing his pizza, and eventually we saw him offering a piece to the two women on his right. I sat there, convinced that he had intentionally ordered a large pizza so as to have a magnet with which to meet women. He seemed to get what he wanted. He was able to engage the women by offering his pizza to them. It only makes sense. Jess wasn't so convinced but I would say he used that pizza as a magnet. After all, the last I glanced after some time, he still had not finished it and he had two other women talking with him. I stand by my theory. Buy the food and the men or women will come.

As easily as food can lure women to your side, excessive drinking can repel them. I had one experience when a man was checking me out by looking my way. Then he began staring. His attention was initially flattering, and then it became a bit annoying and uncomfortable. After a while, he came over and said, "Hi. I know you from somewhere." I replied, "Hmm…I can't say you look familiar." He then goes on, as it turns out, in a drunken slur of words, to tell me he would be interested in having me look at some of his architectural work. I listen, somewhat dumbfounded, and he said, "What's the delay." I let him know I was flattered, but busy and no thank you. He got very frustrated and angry. My friend interjected and reminded him that he didn't even know me. He claimed that it didn't matter. I again reiterated I did not have the time, added that I had a boyfriend, and he still didn't get it.

Sometimes the only way to get rid of a hideous drunk man or woman is to stun them somehow or mention something that, if they were sober, would cause them to run. When the drunken architect asked me what I did. I replied, "I'm a shrink." I chose to answer in this way rather use a less charged word like "counselor," "social worker," or "therapist," because I was hoping to evoke an uncomfortable feeling from him. It happened as I'd predicted. His demeanor changed and he responded in the way I had hoped he would—he became uncomfortable and went on his way. I only wish that sober, normal men would be comfortable when I tell them I am a therapist.

Karaoke night at bars set people up for embarrassment, glory, or some drunken mix of them both. Karaoke can give you a preview of a potential mate's singing voice as well as his or her desire to or fear of being the center of attention. With a few good drinks in them the average Joe can turn into Frank Sinatra. There was one man who I will never forget that I met at Karaoke night at The Bitter. He struck up a conversation with Jess while we were playing pool (of course). Now, this man got really into his Karaoke moment. I'll never forget this man in his mid thirties performing a John Cougar Mellancamp tune. He was a musician by trade and he couldn't resist getting into the Karaoke rotation every couple of songs. During one of his breaks he mentioned his great respect for Madonna and Cyndi Lauper. He said, "Madonna made it okay for men to be sexual and so did Cyndi Lauper. They really made a difference." It was just too classic of a comment to dismiss.

Attire and attitude at bars can start and end conversations easier than in other places. My friend and I once went to a bar known for its margaritas and learned this lesson. We walked in and this man checks me out. I must have been asking for it. I was wearing a hot pink tight tank top with rhinestones. My girlfriend exclaimed, "Girl, he really checked you out." We gave him the once over and I decided he didn't really do it for me. So we went on with our night and worked our way over to another bar.

Soon after our arrival, we ran into the same guy. This time we spoke and he mentioned the previous location and pointed out that he had checked me out. He said my shirt was really making a statement. After all, he was right. We all hung out for a few drinks. One of his friends told me that my demeanor seemed closed and cold and that I didn't seem open or friendly at all. This shocked me because I consider myself to be an open and warm person. His candor was quite valuable to me. I know that although there are benefits to having a closed off "don't fuck with me" look and body language, this may not always be what one wants to portray, especially if one is trying to be open to meeting people. It was, after all, quite an informative night and I owe it to the hot pink shirt.

So, about the bar scene and bar speak…knowing what to do and how to act can be difficult because, on the one hand, you don't want everyone or anyone to approach you, but on the other hand you want to appear open and approachable. I have found that, in general, the men who I want to approach me don't, and those that do approach me are the one's I'm not interested in. It may be that I am attracted to shy, narcissistic or commitment phobic men. I do try to see every situation as different and laugh about it. After all, I don't think people usually go out to a bar with an agenda other than to have fun, get laid, or manage boredom.

The issue of avoiding eye contact at a bar can be tricky. It is a difficult talent to master. My girlfriend Jess and I are regularly spotting those guys we need to avoid eye contact with. One night, for example, we found two great seats at a bar, but they happened to be next to a SLM. She looked to me and muttered, "avoid eye contact" because I was positioned in such a way that I was facing him. I followed her advice. The seating did assist us in that the SLM gave up on talking to us. However, we were bombarded by yet a different man. It was a very interesting approach. He walked up and said, "Hi. I don't want to offend you and I usually wouldn't say anything like this, but I have never in my life seen two women whom I would like to make love to until I saw you two guys here tonight." All we could do was laugh. He turned out to be a drunk, evasive, manipulative, odd person. He left and the SLM attempted to connect with us by discussing the drunken guy who wanted the threesome. Fortunately, it was time to go. Props to both of them for trying anyway.

Is it a coincidence that we have a number of drinks whose names are sexual in nature? I don't think so. The names of many drinks can spark connections. Joy once wanted to order a fuzzy naval. She walked up to the bar and sat in the only empty seat. She ordered her drink and accidentally said "fuzzy nipple" instead of fuzzy navel. The man next to her found this hysterical. Other drink names of interest include the orgasm, the purple hooter, the slow screw against the wall, sex on the beach, and the blowjob. Maybe these names have been invented so as to have an icebreaker or segue into a sexual conversation while inebriated at a bar.

Your "wingman" at a bar can be a key person. A wingman is the man/woman who is there to assist his friends in meeting or hooking up with someone. Ideally, this person is a man who isn't also invested in meeting or hooking up with a woman. Regardless, if one is looking to talk to, meet or impress a woman, a wingman can help. The wingman can advocate for the guy by covertly pointing out his friend's strong points. He can also overtly make positive comments about his friend and give a clear indication that not only is his friend available but that he or his friend is also a catch. I recommend the wingman (or woman) when going out to flirt.

SECTION 2:

SEX

24

ONE-NIGHT STANDS AND SEXUAL ESCAPADES

The one night stand. Such a wonderful, wild, sometimes kinky, free-spirited thing to do. So tempting, so risky, so scandalous, so uncertain, and so scary at times. I must say that I have been smart about it and maybe a bit lucky. As for being safe and using condoms, I have been very good about that. I will make a point here, however, that though people think otherwise, one can still contract sexually transmitted diseases (STD's) while using condoms and people can contract STD's from performing oral sex. This is something to keep in mind. This is where I will do my plug for the flavored condom. There are so many flavors of condoms and they can actually taste pretty good, and not chalky or powdery or plastic-like. Though getting a blowjob through a condom may not feel the same for the giver or the receiver, one needs to think of whether it is worth abandoning the condom and contracting something they may never be able to rid themselves of.

I have had my share of one-night stands and must say that they have been some of the most enjoyable times I've had. I mean, here you meet someone, there is intense sexual energy and an attraction, and both people are just charged up and ready to get down. No strings, just pure sexual, animalistic drive, just down for anything. I am glad that I've been able to experience this. If you haven't had a one-night stand and you are both curious and not yet married, I encourage you to do so if only to minimize the likelihood of cheating on your future partner. This I would encourage only at the level that one is comfortable with the idea and where one has an "itch" that needs to be scratched. Otherwise, I wouldn't be quick to advise it because it could be detrimental.

Not surprisingly, many of my best one-night connections grew out of evenings out with friends at a bar. One night, I ended up talking with this guy from London. He was not really my type, but he caught me at a particularly horny time. I mean *really* horny time. I think I was really charged up during graduate school. So, he and I talked and he brought up sex in the conversation. We start making out, decided to go and "fuck." We actually agreed on doing it. We went back to his house, plastered. He lived about two blocks from me and was the owner of a restaurant/pub I frequented. I felt safe for these reasons. I have good intuition and knew I was taking a risk, but also trusted my instinct that I'd be okay. We had wild, passionate sex all night.

After our night of fun, the Brit pursued me and wanted to develop a dating relationship. I wasn't interested in anything serious with him given that he was ten years older than I and had recently divorced and was an alcoholic. He struck me as very needy and angry. These are often the types of individuals that are attracted to those of us in the helping profession. I felt like the traditional guy rejecting him after an obligatory hang out date following our night of sexual escapades. Aside from our awkward end, I did truly have a blast.

As mentioned earlier about massaging being somewhat of a shoe—in with respect to eventual intercourse or sexual play, dancing can also be a common prelude to the sexual connection. At least for me it is. Dancing is like fucking with clothes on. One of my favorite stories dates back to college. I used to frequent this restaurant, "Jose's," that opened up for dancing and drinking in the later evening hours for dollar drink night on Monday nights.

I would often go to Jose's with my girlfriends, Meliss and Delia. We would dance the night away, flirt, and drink ourselves silly. There was one man in particular, Rocky, whom I saw there almost each time I went. He was HOT, sexy, an extraordinary dancer. I believe there is a direct correlation between dancing and sexual performance. If a person has great rhythm and versatility as a dancer, he or she is most likely an awesome lover. So, I would stare at this hot man. He mesmerized me. I had no shame. I did often see him with a particular group of people, including this one woman. I knew he must be off limits seeing as he was with her so I only admired from afar.

After a few months of this weekly ritual of dancing and drinking at Jose's, not having seen "her" for a while, Rocky and I finally ended up dancing together. He exclaimed, "Where have you been all this time?" and I asked him the same. He told me how great of a dancer I was and I returned the compliment. To make a long story short, we exchanged numbers, hooked up a few nights later and had killer sex. We continued to sleep together for about three months. Now, he wasn't a realistic guy for me to pursue anything serious with, but he had an Italian, surfer-like, bad-boy quality about him that was such a turn on. Ultimately, we parted and I was left feeling awesome having slept with this guy whom I had lusted after for weeks. I have a special fondness for him and for dancing as a means to meeting quality lovers.

Years later, I had another encounter after dancing that proved equally rewarding. I met a couple of guys, Fox and Don, while out dancing with my friend Joy. They had just moved to Los Angeles from Florida. The two of them and I began talking and ended up hanging out all night talking, dancing, and drinking. It was one of those unique connections in which we felt like old friends. It was fun and comfortable and all around great. We all went back to my apartment; they were too intoxicated to drive all the way home. Joy crashed out on the couch. I was left with the two boys, which was okay; we had wine and plenty to talk about. I had drunk a Red Bull at the bar for the first time and didn't realize it might affect me in the way that it did. I was up, without a yawn or anything remotely resembling fatigue until 4:00 in the morning.

After hours of talking and drinking, we decided it was time to go to bed. They were still too drunk to drive home so I let them stay. Joy was still passed out. We decided the guys would sleep in my bed with an agreement that there wouldn't be any play. Well, three people, drinking all night, sexual energy seeping through the air…what would one expect? So, it happened. I had sex with both of them. It was fun. It was late. It was tiresome. The sex didn't alter the dynamic between all of us as much as one might have thought. We all spoke regularly on the phone for a while after that night. We tried to connect again but never did. After a few months, we lost contact.

A year or so later I was out dancing with Darla and Jess and we took a break and had a drink by the bar. There we were, standing there, and whom did I see but Fox. What a trip I thought. I said hello and gave him a hug. He smiled happily, and said a bit awkwardly, "oh my god…I can't remember how I know you." I let him suffer and then finally told him. He claimed that I looked different. Who knows. It had been over a year. Fortunately I have a strong enough ego that I didn't feel hurt that he didn't remember me. However, I think his lapse in memory was a total faux pas.

Another one of my favorite sex tales is that of the Brazilian, Luciano, who I became fixated on while in graduate school. He was a beautiful guy and extremely athletic. I had seen him around here and there. I saw the car he drove, I watched him periodically. I would smile at him. Nothing would ever happen. Finally, I became "ballsy" and left a note on his car saying I thought he was cute and that I wouldn't mind going out some time. He responded to the note. We went out and had a great night. We came back to his dorm room and had great wild sex. Soon thereafter summer break rolled around so we had to go our separate ways. I was left with a great memory of my hot Latin lover and a belief that it can pay off for women to be "ballsy."

I recently heard a female comedian and she broached the always talked about topic of sex, being single, and relationships at large. One thing that really stuck with me that I really liked was with regard to having sex on the first date or soon after two people meet. She said women will then tend to have [an 8 month] relationship with the man after they've done the wild thing so as to not be called or feel like a ho. I think there is some truth to the story. After all, how do we explain, when there don't seem to be deep seated psychological issues, why two people stay together for some time after fucking when they aren't particularly happy together.

One of the best stories I've heard I owe to my friend Sam. Sam is a great wingman and a good friend of mine with whom I have shared a liking for frequenting some variety of places over the past decade. A few years back he went on a business trip. He met this woman at the hotel, they began flirting and one thing led to another and they ended up in her room. So, they have a great night, a lot of fun, great sex and then he realizes he really needs to go. He then jumps up, gets dressed and says, "All right, give me a high five, no, a high 10!" He literally gave her a high ten. I mean, my gosh, can you imagine. He takes the cake for the most humorous exit.

25

THE GENITAL AREA

This chapter is sort of a random variety of stories and scenarios that I felt were worth addressing since the common theme for them all is the genital area. And, let's face it, the genital area is not only an important area, but an area that has shown up in many parts of this book.

My friend Jack has a Harley that he swears is an aphrodisiac and works better for some women than a vibrator. Jack loves his Harley and is convinced that women find pleasure riding on it. A few years back he gave Eve a ride on it around the neighborhood. Last year, Jack, some friends and I ended up talking about that particular night and Jack told me that Eve actually had an orgasm while riding the bike. I called her to see if this had indeed happened, knowing that if it had happened she would have told us at the time. She laughed and said she absolutely did not get herself off while riding the Harley. I told Jack and he said Eve must be too embarrassed to admit it. He said he heard her moan and groan when he had the bike in low gear and high RPM's. Well, I went back and forth between the two of them, and neither of them changed their story. After hearing about this, I was tempted to take a little ride on his Harley. I am glad for Jack though that he has this fantasy and can play it out in his head believing that women enjoy the ride tremendously.

Not long ago, a group of girlfriends of mine and I were painting our nails. One of the women told us that she often gets compliments on how amazing her nails always look. She does do good upkeep. She goes on to tell us that, to maintain nails, one must do everything using the tips of the fingers. We concluded that, to maintain nails, women must be careful when giving a hand job. We all concurred that the palms of the hands must be used carefully, making large strokes, keeping the nails out of the way. If only I could capture the visual. The lesson here is to not let a good old hand job get in the way of a well-done manicure.

Food can enhance any lovemaking, but one must use caution when choosing culinary additions to the bedroom. I know of two women who made dinner using jalapenos for a sauce and then had a great romantic dinner and headed to the bedroom for some nice love making/action. Something was amiss. One of the ladies failed to wash up thoroughly after slicing the jalapenos. Talk about a hot pussy. There her lover was, with stinging peppers all around her vaginal area.

There are a multitude of terms and euphemisms for private parts. Not all of these names should be used during sex though. Jen met a man at a Sierra Club function and they seemed to connect a bit, at least enough to go on a date or two. He was a gynecologist. She and I couldn't help but wonder why a man would want to become a gynecologist. In one of our conversations I asked her what she could do with her legs spread other than ask, "do you want to check me for a vaginal infection or eat me out." They didn't last long. He didn't help his cause any by using gentle medical terminology when they talked dirty. He would say "bottom" and "penis" and she felt like more of a patient than a sex object. No fun.

Speaking of terminology, there are a few occasions when using technical terms can be appropriate while discussing sexual experiences. I learned this lesson with Jan. She had explored her attraction for women, but wasn't ready to talk about it yet. She was a bit sensitive about her sexual orientation and was a bit confused. Seven of us women friends were together swapping stories of whom we were dating, who we were doing, etc. Because Jan was a tad shy sexually she was reticent about details of her experiences with the woman. She said, "Why don't you guys just ask me specific questions about it?" So, I took the ball and asked, "Well, was there digital stimulation?" The entire table broke out in laughter. She chuckled and said yes. Fortunately, neither of them had been preparing jalapenos. Though very technical, my question did get Jan talking about her sexual experiences. Following that conversation, my friends and I have jokingly referred to any incident including fooling around with the question: "was there any digital stimulation?"

The shape and appearance of my genital area is an ongoing challenge for me. I have altered my pubic hair using every treatment known to man. Once I had both shaved and used *Nair* hair remover around my vaginal area. I didn't apply *Nair* to the whole area, but I did get it close to my labia. I had sex with the man I was dating at the time and when we were done we noticed that my lips were quite large. Knowing my lips swell when I am really turned on, I wasn't that concerned. But, I did notice that they were particularly huge that night.

Hours passed, more sex, more hours and the following day I awoke with what appeared to be a penis growing between my legs. My labia were so large that I felt them hanging down and I thought they might even rub up against my legs. It was so bad and scary that I had to show Joy and Lizbeth. Looking back, it was an amusing situation. I went to the doctor, got anti-inflammatory medicine, and iced myself. I wore skirts, spread my legs while sitting and standing as much as possible, and my lips shrunk down after a couple of days. I still don't know if the *Nair* caused the reaction or if I had an allergic reaction to something, shaved improperly, or had a reaction to the latex condom.

I don't think that my scary labia (a.k.a. temporary mini penis) reaction is nearly as bad as a situation an ex-boyfriend of mine once had. He got poison oak on and around his penis. We had been out hiking and we messed around. Within an hour his dick was swelling and itching from poison oak exposure. This just goes to show you how careful you need to be in the wilderness. If a guy urinates or jacks off or adjusts after playing in the woods, he must either scrub down his hands with anti-bacterial soap or use some form of cloth to cover the genital area.

One must also be careful when going commando (not wearing underwear). I sometimes don't wear underwear. Once I went roller blading while going commando. I put on a pair of stretch pants made of cotton and went on my way. It was a bit chilly. I had a good ride, came home, and sat on the steps of my apartment. I leaned down to unlace one of my skates and I saw there was a piece of bubble gum stuck to my pants near my crotch. Not only was it stuck there, but it had some hair on it. I thought, how the hell could there be bubble gum on my pants…I was roller blading, not rolling in the grass. I was about to lean down and remove it when I realized it was not a piece of hairy bubble gum but rather my lips sticking out of a hole in my pants. It then dawned on me why it had felt so chilly there. I started to chuckle to myself. In sharing this story with a couple of my girlfriends, we all got quite a laugh out of that story. I am sure the guys skating behind me enjoyed the show. I ended up throwing the pants away.

I had the same chance to chuckle at my misfortune in another situation in which I found a hole in my pants. I was at Sasha's birthday at a restaurant/pool hall place playing pool. She leaned over and told me that I had a hole in my pants. I mean, my gosh. Thank God I wasn't going commando that night so nothing could actually be seen. I leaned over to make a shot, and exposed the hole, giving everyone a laugh. After all, the group there was really just a group of her friends so I wasn't too embarrassed. Ever since these two incidents I have been particularly careful about the pants I wear and have checked vigilantly whether they have a hole in them.

For those people who have not heard of a "High T" person, I think this a good place to mention it. Basically, there are people who have higher levels of testosterone than others. This is no surprise. All men and women have varying testosterone levels. Those that have higher testosterone levels, the "High Ts", usually have more hair on their bodies. In addition, they have a higher sex drive than others and often experience deeper orgasms. So, if you're concerned about a partner's libido, one way to determine if they are a "High T" is by checking out the amount of hair they have.

26

SLEEPING WITH FRIENDS

What is it about having sex with friends, those "friends with benefits?" I would have to say that there seem to be clear advantages and serious disadvantages to sleeping with friends. Back in college I experimented in this area and slept with a few friends. I lived with a male roommate my third year of college. He was someone I had known from my dorm the year prior. He was a great guy, we got along well, and we were quite compatible roommates.

Throughout our time of living together, we had open discussions about sexuality. He was just as open as I. He was a great masseuse. We also discussed swapping massages. Finally we followed through and gave each other massages. I am convinced that massaging is always a sure way to get into someone's pants. Receiving massages can be a very sensual experience and such a turn on that I believe willpower goes down the tubes never to be seen again. So, one evening, he gave me a massage, took my clothes off, complimented me, and we are both definitely turned on. He told me that he was very turned on and wanted to relieve himself. He asked if I would like to watch. I said yes. I mean, how could I resist. After all, I had only watched a guy jerk off a couple of times before and I was all about learning new things. I laid back and watched. We never had sex. The best part of the story, however, is that he jerked off into a macaroni and cheese box. I have never seen macaroni and cheese in the same light since, over ten years later.

Sleeping with an ex's friends usually is a really bad idea but it can work out. A number of years after one of my ex's, Ray, and I had stopped dating, I maintained a friendship with his friend, Harrison. Harrison and I always had a good time together. We had discussed a sexual attraction existing between us. He had told Ray that he was curious about me, but, at that time, I think we were both involved with other people. Well, after many years had gone by, I went to visit him in Northern California during one serious of my breaks from graduate school. I spent the night and was given the living room. After a bit of awkwardness, we were able to manipulate the situation such that I joined him in his bed.

We were both turned on and had some sexual play, some mutual masturbation, and both got off. It was great. We talked about it the next morning. This was refreshing to be able to essentially "check-in" with one another about our experience because often times one can't. I have wondered what would have happened if we ever lived in the same city. After all, we are good friends, have known each other for years, and we are attracted to one another.

Harrison, on the next trip I made up north, orchestrated a reunion with his ex-girlfriend, Anastasia and us. She and I had been friends for a couple of years back in college. He also let me in on a secret she had told him. She had been attracted to me back in college. After college she explored her attraction to women, and identified herself as bisexual. She shared with him that she had had fantasies about me. I was flattered and curious. After all, I was open to experimenting. We each had hinted openly that we might engage in some threesome type of activity during this "reunion." He ended up having to go home and she and I were left together for the night. She took me all over San Francisco and we talked about our curiosity and fantasy of being together. We ended the night back at her house, and had a wonderful night of sex. Now, Harrison regrets that he didn't stay out with us for the duration of the evening. I haven't talked to her since shortly after that time.

I am of the opinion that being sexual with a friend can be extraordinary and positive. You already have a basic level of comfort and respect with a friend, and there are fewer unknowns than with a stranger. I believe that if your partner is a safe person, and you are both single and sexually frustrated, why not? There are potential disadvantages though. Friends often get emotionally involved when they become intimate. Emotions can get in the way or confuse what is primarily a physical experience. The question then becomes whether or not both people can handle the situation emotionally. I think, at times, one or the other person is left wondering why the friendship can't develop into a love relationship if all of the ducks are in a row. I will say that as much as sleeping with friends has been a safe and comfortable way of satisfying myself sexually, it somehow has felt less and less appealing over time.

Not long ago, I had a couple of old girlfriends from high school in town. We all went out for coffee and began to reminisce. It was great. This led to sex stories and who had messed around with whom. We started to realize that there was a lot of overlap from over the years. As we talked more and more, I pulled out a pen and paper and drew up a diagram of those who'd been with the same person and such. Anyone who was paying any attention to us at that coffee shop must've really gotten a thrill. I'm talking about eight women who had all shared at least one man at some point over the past 15 years! One of the women had been with 7 of the men a combination of the others had been with! Don't try this at home! It could be dangerous. I'll be certain to hide this list from my future husband.

SECTION 3:

MARRIAGE

27

WEDDINGS

Weddings can be such a wonderful experience for guests, while at the same time they can be uncomfortable, frustrating, and sickening for a single guest. Judging by the variety of conversations I have had about weddings with people, I believe that women are more affected by going to weddings than men.

I have had an exhilarating time at a couple of weddings, and I have also had a horrible time. The disaster weddings were no fault of the bride or groom, rather the circumstances, environment, and how I was relating to being single at the time.

Starting with the good, there are two weddings in particular that stand out as truly great experiences. They also happened to be just one week apart from one another so the whole month was a good one for matrimony. The first wedding included quite a cultural mix. The bride's side of the family tends to party a lot. I think her family and guests enjoyed drinking at the wedding, while the groom's Mormon family didn't drink at all. So, suffice to say there was quite a mix. I was a close friend of the bride and of one of her bridesmaids. As a guest of the bride, it was only logical that I party hard.

The main reason I had such a blast at the wedding was the serious ego boost I got at the reception. I was repetitively complimented on the dress I wore for the reception. The highlight of the night for me was hearing the excellent disco-cover band. They dedicated a couple of songs to me. It may have helped that they were friends with the bride. Who wouldn't be stoked if *Brick House* was specifically dedicated to them at a wedding in front of a number of people?

I learned later that the lead singer was interested in me. He was a bit shy but that didn't stop us from ultimately talking. After the wedding we all went dancing at a club and had a great time…again I got a lot of compliments about my dress, dancing ability, and what not. It just was one of those "on" nights in which I was really feeling good and flattered. EVERYONE should be able to have this experience. The attraction between the singer and I added to the joy of the evening. I felt like that lucky girl in the story of the "LEAD singer (OH MY GOD!) likes me" syndrome. One of my guy friends says women get "LV disease"—lead vocalist disease. I certainly had it that night…so, I took him home and we had a great time.

The next wedding was a great deal of fun because it was like a high school reunion. A close guy friend of mine married a woman he'd been dating for a while. The groom and I have many mutual friends. The wedding was great—a lot of dancing, drinking, gabbing, and eating. I think it's a good thing the wedding took place before our high school reunion because I actually had a lot more quality conversations with the people at the wedding than I did at the reunion. It helped that the couple had good taste in music and that I was sitting near the wedding party with his best man/brother, a good friend of mine.

Unfortunately, I have more negative experiences to share than positives, and I hope this does change in the future. One aspect which I think is of note is the issue of alcohol. I have friends who are sober or don't drink or who are in recovery. I also happen to know that alcohol can sometimes be helpful in terms of relaxing, loosening up, being less self-analytical, calming down, or caring less. Well, I like alcohol at weddings, straight up.

The only wedding, thus far, that I've been in was a sober wedding. One person is in recovery and the other doesn't drink. Fortunately, I knew a few people at the wedding. I thought, no problem, I'm in the wedding, I know a couple of people, I like to dance, and the bride is one of my best friends. Well, the ceremony itself was beautiful and pleasant. No problem. The reception on the other hand was extremely difficult. I was one of two people in the bridal party (the other being her younger sister) sitting at a different table than the bridal party. What's up with that? It was the "odd ball table," the table of "randoms"…lovely. Then, on top of it, I'm seated next to her sister, bless her heart, who is a very sweet and engaging person. But, her level of energy, anxiety and talkativeness was rather annoying. So, there I was, no booze, no really close friend, no date, out of town, next to an anxious and neurotic person with a bunch of random, single odd-balls. Yuck! At least the pictures turned out well and I wasn't forced to wear some peach shiny faux silk gown with bows on it.

Another out of town wedding I attended with a friend of mine was equally horrible. I took Jen as my date, but she had to leave after the appetizer. Lovely, I thought. I figured that at least by the time she left I would have acclimated, met some people, and felt comfortable. Well, quite the contrary. I did not know a soul. Jen and I were seated at, you guessed it, a table with all couples and married people. Ironically, after the meal, the bride, a friend I'd had for fifteen years, comes over to say her hello's to the table and exclaims, "Did you see that group over there of all the single men...you should talk to them!" I thought, dear God, is this woman high? Why didn't she think of this prior and why did she seat me with these people? I basically ate and left. No reason to remain. The group at the table consisted of a Caucasian middle class engaged couple who could not keep their hands off one another, two married women who came together, and a very quiet couple who had nothing to say. I even found myself making attempts to engage in conversation to no avail. The table was boring, quiet, self-absorbed, and extremely uncomfortable. I literally felt I couldn't find a single topic in common with these people.

I had another bad case of wedding discomfort happen out of state at a wedding in Ohio. Out of state weddings can be a big problem. You really have nowhere to go. A few months before the wedding, the bride-to-be and I talked, and in her efforts to help me meet Mr. Right, she mentioned a guy who lived in Los Angeles whom she thought would be a real catch and who was a good friend of her fiancée's. She explained to me that he would be in the wedding so that I could be on my toes and check him out there. It also turns out that my friend Lisa would be attending the wedding with her husband, Mark. So, I figure, this is all good and exciting. I will have friends there, potentially a man I can at least flirt with, and I will have become pretty acquainted with the bridal party seeing as I'll be sharing a room with them and hanging with them at the bachelorette party.

Ironically, it turns out that the bachelorette party was a blast, seeing as the wedding had been quite the contrary. I had never been to one before and had nothing to compare it to, but it was just a great old time. Again, a disco cover band. What is it with these disco cover bands? The bridal party played all sorts of practical jokes and placed phallic symbols on virtually everything. The bride wore a corsage on her blouse. It was not a normal corsage, but rather a PENIS so extraordinarily realistic that I wish I could have taken one home myself. It had hair, testicles, and the whole thing. Of course, the penis corsage was a conversation piece.

The best part of the evening was the bride's blow up penis, which, must have been about 8 feet tall and 2 feet in diameter. We schlepped the penis around to various places and the penis turned out to get more attention than we did. Maybe my recommendation here should be to carry around a large penis if you're looking to meet a man. Now, unfortunately, the FAMILY-style restaurant where we ate (God knows who picked this for a bridal shower) didn't appreciate this and we had to place the damn thing is a broom closet. We began our night there, eating, gabbing, and enjoying various drinks with sexual names. Something quite pleasurable about the evening was that the bride-to-be was not a big drinker so she was easily intoxicated, and quite humorous when she was.

After we left the restaurant, we trolled around the city, bar hopped, and had such a great time. I was convinced afterward that, not only should I have one of these blow up penises with me at my future bridal shower, but that I should really consider carrying one around on a regular basis. I mean, I don't think any of us had been approached by so many men at a given time. It was such a man magnet. So, I guess the hysterical bachelorette party balanced out the difficulty and challenge of the wedding.

After the bachelorette party, it was back to the hotel. Sharing a hotel room with strangers is always a bit odd. I guess you could say that I am not very modest around women. This is just the way I was raised and this is how most of my women friends are (men, get your tongues back in your mouth). But, the three women I shared a room with were all modest, changing in the bathroom and what not. They were not too modest to lug around an eight-foot penis in public, but changing pants in front of another woman was too risqué for them.

Changing around other women can be a weird scenario in that one wonders what one is supposed to do: copy them or do your own thing at the risk of being judged. I think I did a modification of both. So, additionally, because I was the random person, not from the bride's hometown as these other three women were, it was not totally comfortable. The icing on the cake was that I was been exhausted the last night there. While everyone hung out in another hotel room after the wedding reception, I left to go to sleep. My roommates returned, loud as hell, drunk as hell, and had no respect for yours truly, trying to catch some Z's. I couldn't help but wonder if there was some warped intention behind this careless act.

Regarding the aforementioned man from L.A., I missed out on that Mr. Right. When I got to the rehearsal dinner, I hung out with the couple of women I was going to room with. I then saw this woman I knew, but couldn't place. I thought, "Who is she?" You know, that instance where you're trying to make some connection and can't. Finally, it hit me, she was a friend of a couple of friends of mine in L.A. We said hello, caught up a bit, and she introduced me to her boyfriend. He looked a bit familiar and then, something else hit me. He was the guy the bride had mentioned to me months earlier in L.A., and he was a friend of our mutual friends. What a bust. Small world. So, at least someone swiped him up.

The wedding itself was beautiful, as was the reception…until Lisa and Mark left. Lovely, I thought, here I am, alone, once again, watching this beautiful bride and groom, so happy, and the couple from L.A. who were dancing and laughing. Meanwhile I sat with a bunch of couples and a nerdy uncomfortable husband of one of the bridesmaids. The only thing I had going for me was that there was good food and booze. Otherwise, I was absolutely miserable. I had all of these thoughts…wondering when I was going to be a bride and wondering why it was so damn difficult for me. I was three years older than this bride. C'est la vie…I took comfort in the fact that I only had a couple more days until I would home. The lesson I learned here is that I should never go out of state to a wedding unaccompanied.

The most recent hellish experience I had was when I went to a wedding of a dear male friend of mine who I have known for about twenty years, Andrew. He and I met at an overnight camp that we both went to for years and ultimately worked at. So, you can imagine that the wedding was to consist of many people whom I'd known for a number of years. I was excited to go because it seemed that the wedding would be comparable to the fun, high school reunion-like wedding from three years prior. This was only partly true.

The glitch at Andrew's wedding was that I brought Tyler. I had been dating him for about a month and a half. Things were moving fast and comfortably so I felt inclined to invite him. This was a horrible idea. Jack also attended the wedding. Jack and I had had sex intermittently over the course of the previous five years. When neither of us were involved in a relationship and were both feeling sexual, we acted on the desire. Essentially, if someone is a friend and there is an agreement, it feels safe, and comfortable, then why not? Better than a random stranger or being so horny after being sexually deprived for five years.

The last encounter Jack and I had happened to be after I had my first date with Tyler. One date only. At the time of our date, Tyler was separated from his girlfriend of 3 and ½ years. He and I spent a great deal of the conversation processing their separation. I had no way of knowing where our connection was going to go, nor was there anything remotely like a commitment between us. I had also already planned the group trip on which Jack and I hooked up.

Being as honest as I am, when Tyler casually asked about my trip when I returned, I was honest with him. I had told him I'd gone skinny dipping in the sea with my friends and he, point blank, asked if I'd had sex. I gave him the whole history. He was quite uncomfortable with my response. Unbeknownst to me at the time, he had a more conservative view about sex than I. He said he couldn't understand the idea of being sexual with a person who wasn't a committed partner. Looking back, maybe it wasn't such a good idea to be as honest as I was. Maybe, however, it was very telling of our differences and meant to be discussed.

The subject of sleeping with friends came up again at the wedding when Tyler put 2 and 2 together and figured out who Jack was. Now, it is important to mention here that I had chosen not to tell Tyler that Jack was going to be at the wedding because I didn't want him to feel uncomfortable. I was not hiding or lying, but rather trying to protect him. My plan totally backfired. Tyler threw a tantrum at the wedding and completely wigged out. This was the first sign of our dating relationship being doomed. So, the lesson here is not to bring an insecure person whom you've just started dating to a wedding where partners from the past will be.

I have also gone to weddings as the date of an invited guest. I have vivid memories of one wedding in particular that I went to as a date. I was about 21 years old, had just graduated from college. My friend, Harrison, was to be one of the groom's men in the wedding. He asked me to accompany him, in part because he was driving to the wedding and it was a long trip from northern California to Seattle. And, additionally he asked me because I happened to have the time to spare. So, off we went.

Basically, on the night of the bachelor party, I was left on my own in the hotel room, in a rainy city without a car, and didn't know when to expect his return. Well, I was bored out of my mind and I think, because I was still a young chicken, I wasn't able to maximize my down time. I did feel there was something about me being a guest and not feeling as well taken care of as I should've been. I figured things might improve at the wedding. Well, this turned out not to be the case. The wedding was Catholic and I had never attended a Catholic wedding before. I thought I was going to end up with black and blue knees. Sit, kneel, stand. Sit, kneel, stand. It sure was a workout. I was also bored out of my mind. The only person I knew, having met him only once or twice before, was the groom. Great, I thought. I was left to be on my own after the ceremony during the reception. Not a good scenario. I don't know if the lesson is to not go as a guest to a wedding when you know no one or not to go as a guest if the person you're accompanying is in the wedding party and you have no getaway car.

As an aside, I once went to a wedding with my friend Jeff as a favor to him. Guess what the problem was? Everyone thought we were a couple. This was not at all the case but the guests all assumed we were. After a while I felt as though I should be wearing a sign saying, "we are just friends." The lesson is: do not expect to pick up anyone if you go to a wedding as your friend's date.

Lastly, I do have a funny story about Jan's wedding, which happens to be the most recent one I've attended. She planned the seating at her wedding reception with the idea that the young single women sit near the young single men. So, in her efforts to do this, I was to sit with a single woman whom I did not know and who was there alone, two single men, and two couples. Basically, I was left attempting to calculate where I would sit such that I would not be stuck next to both sets of couples. Sherry, her boyfriend and I assessed and evaluated the variety of combinations and ways we could arrange our seating. Strategizing our seating game plan was hysterical.

Ultimately, we made a decision that I would sit between the two single guys and next to Sherry. Neither of the single men turned out to be of interest to me after all. In one sense all of our conniving was for naught. However, the strenuous effort was worth it if only because my friends and I were entertained by, and consumed with manipulating such a minor thing as the seating arrangement. I guess you could say that I have had sufficient experience with weddings to know that it is worth putting in a little extra neurotic effort in order to avoid the frustration and boredom of a bad seating arrangement.

The last tidbit regarding the wedding theme is something that happened as I was writing this book. I received an invitation from my friend Katarina that said, "So and so request the honor of your presence as they renew their vows in celebration of their Tenth Year Anniversary." What the hell is that? Isn't it enough they have one wedding? Why is it that they feel the need to rub it in other's faces that they are so happy they want to marry again. It is hard enough for me to go to regular weddings. Now, I'm stuck with a ten-year anniversary. What's next?

28

COUPLES

Because I have covered weddings, it seems logical here to address the aftermath of the wedding—the married couple. Couple dynamics are exemplified in many different areas of a couple's home life. One example of this is the answering machine. I believe that the individual who is in power or more controlling and "wears the pants" is the person whose voice is on the machine. Of course, there are couples who choose to have their children record messages on the answering machine and get a kick out of it. I wonder if we could speculate that indeed this means that the couple's status is more egalitarian. It is hard to say. Though there is no hard evidence here, I do suggest that you look at the couples you know and notice whose voice is on the machine. Now, ask yourself who wears the pants.

Additionally, is there a rule about whose name is earlier in the alphabet or more rhythmic sounding. What sounds better? Mark and Joanne or Joanne and Mark? Or Heather and Fred or Fred and Heather? I have a friend whose boyfriend tends to wear the pants a bit more than she, so he, of course, is on the answering machine. On the machine, however, he says his name before hers even though alphabetically his comes after hers. Maybe there is no rule or pattern after all.

Recently, I was conversing with Jennifer who chose to heed the advice from another friend. That was the concept of surrounding oneself by others that represented what she wanted. So, in essence, if, as a single woman, Jennifer was hoping to transform into a woman who was in a loving relationship, then she should place herself in this environment. Of course, what continues to come to my mind is the saying, "you are what you eat." Additionally, if one spends time at events with couples, it is likely that the couples themselves will have, you guessed it, couples or people interested in such. Concluded on her part was that it is better to hang out with couples than singles in terms of accessibility and environment.

29

RELATIONSHIPS

How much should one disclose on a first date, and at what point should one disclose information that may be of a sensitive nature? When and why do people commit, and when should they? How much disclosure do you need to have on a previous relationship before beginning another one? These are all valuable questions.

My friend Liz said to her now husband on their first date, "I know I want to get married and have kids and I don't want to waste time by dating someone who doesn't want what I want. I don't know what will happen with us but I just don't want to fuck around." He agreed to date her. Now, I must admit that, though it is coming on strong, I do like this approach. It's direct and to the point. There are no games involved, and each person can learn where the other person stands and what they expect from a date. Unfortunately, this level of direct communication is rare. Consequently, such candor can frighten people.

The running theme, however, I personally have experienced in the dating world is that men are often not "looking for a serious relationship" but rather are looking just to date. I have operated with the mentality that if a man seems to have issues with commitment, then I end the relationship. I now realize that if someone <u>appears</u> to have commitment issues, I should give it time before I determine the person is incapable of commitment. Maybe it isn't so black and white. I can think of, literally, ten couples who are happy and committed. In each of these couples, the man had appeared non-committal. I do believe that some men and women are simply incapable of commitment, but some people simply haven't opened themselves to committing to another person.

A person just has to be in the right place at the right time and their light has to be on. Maybe they will see the merits of committing after some time has passed and if the other party is patient. Always looking at the depth of feelings is important. On the other hand, it may be possible that the two halves of the couple just don't feel the same way. The two people might not be a match and despite whether the light is on or not, they aren't meant to be together. Maybe there is just that chemical connection that is either there or not. Maybe one person is aware of how incompatible the two are, but is choosing to focus on having the so-called "commitment issues" instead. Or, he may be clueless about the fact that the feelings are just not mutual. There are a variety of possibilities and one needs to be aware of this despite how tempting it can be to make generalizations.

I always advocate for closure because I feel it is so important. If a potential partner still references their past partner and doesn't seem to be over them, this should be a warning sign and a red flag, or red light, if you will. People need time to grieve a lost partner and a failed relationship under all circumstances. I promote time even when the relationship ends badly, or you desire and initiate the break-up. Often people underestimate the importance of the grieving process. It depends on the person and the length and depth of the relationship as to how long one needs to grieve. I have heard one method of determining how long it takes and it seems to work for some. Some say it takes half the length of time that a person was dating someone to get over them. That seems unfortunate if the relationship was long term, but not too bad if it was brief.

I do have a suggestion and that is to be aware of times in which you feel as though you are bonding with someone because you are talking or commiserating, or even almost counseling someone, about a previous relationship that ended not long ago. I learned this the hard way. You do not want to be a rebound. One can get trapped into the delusion that there is a bond when two people do discuss the ex's; the reality is that the person is venting and the attraction felt toward the person venting translates to support and an alliance. However, when one begins to talk a great deal about the ex in the beginning and they are drawing frequent comparisons between the two of you, they should be asked to stop. When the preoccupation resides with a previous lover/partner, this is cause for a lot of potential torment and it stinks. Watch out.

So, in sum, if you desire a loving, lengthy partnership, the people to avoid are the following: red light men or women, those who clearly do not want a commitment, those who express a lot of uncertainty as to what they hope for in the future, people who have just ended a relationship, people who seem dishonest about their past, and people with whom you feel sex is the most important aspect of the relationship or where sex is the only focus.

An issue that surfaces regularly in relationships is how to disclose touchy issues and when to disclose them. I can think of two instances in particular where I had to tiptoe around certain topics and delicately negotiate the timing of highly charged topics.

I think it's best told as a story. When Tyler and I went on our first date, we fooled around. There was some strong sexual chemistry between us that became a bit of a problem in the long run. Who would have known? Great sexual chemistry is an important aspect of a relationship to me, but with Tyler, it couldn't save us and it distorted things.

We also had a conversation, early on, about ménage a trois. I told him that I'd had one and he was intrigued (what a surprise) and curious and asked if I'd have one again. I told him that I had no interest in doing so, but that if it was really important to my mate, or was a fantasy that a man I was involved with seriously very much wanted, then I would consider it again. But, I explained, that I had gotten it out of my system and satisfied my curiosity.

Tyler had also never gotten over the fact that I had sex with Jack on my trip following the very first date I had with him. Throughout our relationship, Tyler commented that he didn't know if I'd just "fuck" a friend in the future and he said repeatedly that he couldn't understand, no matter how hard he tried, why or how I could do that when sex was so sacred. He actually, at one point, said to me he wasn't sure if I was interested in women or not. As if to say that I was a lesbian. So, we continued to date and my honesty ultimately bit me in the ass.

I found Tyler's criticism hypocritical coming from a man who didn't act like sex was sacred. He wanted to film a porn video (and did so with yours truly), and was interested in screwing in the brush while on a hike, was really kinky and loved spanking. He enjoyed a periodic blowjob while on the freeway, and he once virtually stripped me down in the car one time while I was driving, fingering me all the while, for a full thirty-minute car ride. I won't deny that I was into all of it; I'm pretty kinky myself. But, what I will say is that his criticism reflected such a double standard. He loved and relished the fact that I am so sexual, yet he judged me for my sexuality.

I think, though, the point is to be sensitive to the issue of how much to disclose at the beginning of a relationship. Use honesty and discretion when discussing your sexual past. It is best to not say something or share about something that may threaten another person. The fact that I had slept with a male friend who was still in my life was very threatening to Tyler. And, remember that your value system and past relationships might be very different from your partner's. For instance, I know other men in my life who would not have judged me in the same way.

Interestingly, Shane asked what had happened with Tyler on our first date. I spared him all the details but told him that I'd told Tyler about having had a threesome and how he was intrigued initially, but later judged me and used it against me. Shane smiled and was truly shocked at Tyler's response. He said he thought my rich sex life was cool and said, "I have material for five nights, are you kidding?" I am certain his tolerance was part of the reason I liked Shane. I took a risk by being so open with him, but it didn't backfire. I just know I should ideally be a bit more selective about when and how I discuss my sexuality. No one wants to be prejudged, perceived negatively or mistaken for someone they are not.

Best put is that one should be cognizant of the fine line between being patient and not pressuring another person with respect to timing and commitment and making a lot of personal sacrifices to avoid appearing as if they are placing a lot of pressure on another person.

30

BENEFITS TO BEING ALONE OR TO NOT BEING COMMITTED

I recently went with Sasha and Jess on a bike ride and we discussed the relationship issue and how we felt being single. In my frustration, I said that it is difficult to fathom being alone indefinitely. They both encouraged me to do something they'd both informally done for themselves: write a list of what the benefits to being alone are (or can be). I suggest those who share any frustration as I have in the past might benefit from doing the same. So, here was the list I created about what being alone can provide me with:

1. Freedom I wouldn't have otherwise

2. Responsibility only for myself

3. Financial freedom

4. A chance to make any choices I wish

5. An opportunity to move if I wish

6. A chance to vacation wherever and whenever I want

7. The possibility of dating a number of people

8. A chance to be sexual with a lot of different men

9. The opportunity to meet and spend time with more people

10. I can achieve greater successes

11. I don't have to deal with fights, conflicts, or arguments

12. I won't have to lose someone to death or their choice of leaving

13. I don't have to deal with someone telling me what to do

14. I won't have to shave

15. I don't' have to gain weight from bearing a child

16. I can work on my independence and anxiety levels further

17. I can exercise more

18. I never have to pick a house based on the local school district

CONCLUSION

In summary, I suggest you ask yourself some preliminary questions before entering a relationship. Heeding my own advice, one day Joy and I discussed our woes—we had both lost men with whom we'd hoped a relationship would last. During this long day, over a few *Hefenweizens*, we decided to develop a list of questions to ask a man before we felt we were ready to date them. You might not want to try this at home, or not all at once anyway. This is not to be taken so literally that you bombard a man (ladies) or woman (non-commitment-phobic men), but to consider if ultimately you are looking for love and maintaining it. This is what we came up with:

1. Do you want a commitment?

2. Are you sure you want a commitment?

3. Are you ready for a commitment now?

4. Are you content being alone?

5. Are you sure you understand what a commitment *needs*?

6. Are you comfortable expressing a full range of feelings?

7. Have you gotten over your ex?

8. If you have been to therapy, has it been useful?

9. Are you comfortable being romantic?

10. Do you understand what a woman needs?

11. Are you able to be honest with yourself and others?

12. Have you experienced healthy communication in a relationship before?

13. Are you clear about what you're looking for in a woman?

14. Do you have an idea about what your future looks like?

15. Do you have friends who you can confide in or who you have support from?

16. Are you able to give what it takes to maintain a relationship?

17. Are you able and willing to meet someone half way?

18. Are you comfortable disclosing your age?

19. Is it hard for you to trust people?

20. Do you like or want pets?

Once you've answered these questions for yourself and are ready, enjoy the process, reach out when you need the support, and best of luck to you. In the mean time, consider the various elements of dating, both good and bad, and stay as positive as you can. Give yourself a break when you need it and never forget that you aren't alone. There is always another person with whom you can relate. And, lastly, if you are not specifically in search of that "love" relationship now or don't expect you ever will be, may you relish in your sexual escapades! But, never forget to practice "safer" sex!

0-595-29257-7

www.ingramcontent.com/pod-product-compliance
Lightning Source LLC
Chambersburg PA
CBHW020246290526
45784CB00003B/1115